THE

Cutter's Practical Guide

TO

CUTTING AND MAKING

JUVENILE GARMENTS

Bibliografische Information der Deutschen Nationalbibliothek:
Die Deutsche Nationalbibliothek verzeichnet diese Publikation
in der Deutschen Nationalbibliografie; detaillierte bibliografische
Daten sind im Internet über www.dnb.de abrufbar.

Reprint of the original from 1890
© 2025
Republished by Sven Jungclaus
https://www.becomeatailor.com

Verlag:
BoD · Books on Demand GmbH, In de Tarpen 42,
22848 Norderstedt, bod@bod.de
Druck:
Libri Plureos GmbH, Friedensallee 273, 22763 Hamburg
ISBN: 978-3-7693-2515-7

THE CUTTERS'
PRACTICAL GUIDE

TO CUTTING EVERY KIND OF

GARMENT MADE BY TAILORS,

IN A SERIES OF PARTS.

Part One.

YOUNG MEN'S, YOUTHS'

AND

JUVENILE GARMENTS.

EMBRACING ALSO TREATISE ON

Trousers, Vests, Military Garments, Liveries,

&c., &c., &c.

BY W. D. F. VINCENT.

*Author of " The Federation First Prize Essay on Trouser Cutting," " The First Prize Essay on the
Management of Foremen Tailor Societies," &c., &c., and*

One of the Teachers at the " Tailor and Cutter " School of Art, 93 and 94 Drury Lane, London, W.C.

PRICE FIFTEEN SHILLINGS.

PRINTED AND PUBLISHED BY THE JOHN WILLIAMSON COMPANY LIMITED,
AT *THE TAILOR AND CUTTER* OFFICE, 93 & 94 DRURY LANE, LONDON, W.C.

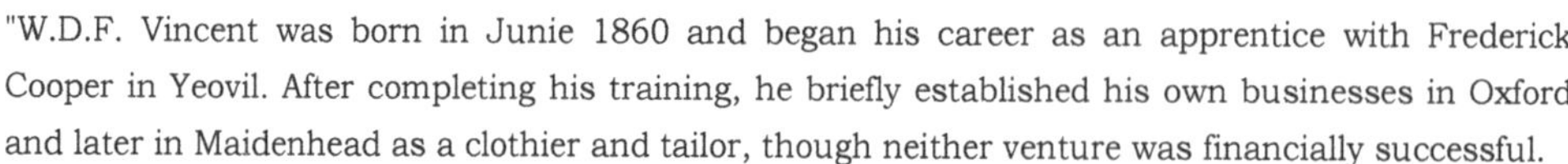

"W.D.F. Vincent was born in Junie 1860 and began his career as an apprentice with Frederick Cooper in Yeovil. After completing his training, he briefly established his own businesses in Oxford and later in Maidenhead as a clothier and tailor, though neither venture was financially successful.

While in Maidenhead, Vincent won an essay competition on tailoring, which was open to all members of the National Federation of Foremen Tailors, titled "The Great National Work on Trouser Cutting, or Defects in Trousers." He submitted his entry under the pseudonym "Oxonian" and won the first prize. This success led him to secure a position with The Tailor and Cutter magazine. In the early years, Vincent contributed numerous articles on tailoring methods and techniques to the magazine. However, due to the terms of his employment, these articles were published without attribution to him.

By the 1890s, Vincent became a leading tailoring authority. His books, such as The Cutter's Practical Guide to the Cutting & Making of All Kinds of Trousers, became standard reference work. By 1917, Vincent referred to himself as a journalist. He died in June 1926.

The Tailor and Cutter magazine and academy were operated by John Williamson & Co Ltd. In the 1950s and 1960s, many tailors displayed their Tailor & Cutter Academy Diplomas, signed by W.D.F. Vincent, as the Chairman of Examiners, as a centerpiece in their shop windows. One such example can still be seen on display at the Museum of Welsh Life at St. Fagans in South Wales."

(cf. https://vincents.org.uk/family-history/w-d-f-vincent-tailor; 15.12.2024)

This edition is a reprint of the legendary *Cutter's Practical Guide* series; the first book was published in 1890. Although W. D. F. Vincent wrote many books on tailoring, these are the most popular. The entire text has been meticulously read, and the images have been carefully cleaned and edited to ensure the highest quality.

Part 1 – Juvenile Garments
Part 2 – Body Coats
Part 3 – Trousers, Breeches & Knickers
Part 4 – Livery Garments in all their varieties
Part 5 – Overcoats
Part 6 – Ladies' Garments
Part 7 – Defects, Remedies, Trying on & The Art of Fitting
Part 8 – Economical Cutting
Part 9 – Lounges, Reefers, Norfolk, Sporting & Patrol Jackets
Part 10 – Waistcoats for Gentlemen, Ladies, Military & Naval Officers, etc.
Part 11 – Shirts, Undergarments, Collars, Cuffs, Aprons, etc.
Part 12 – Clerical Dress
Part 13 – British Military Uniforms

Content

AUTHOR'S PREFACE

I t is with some degree of pleasure I look upon this, the first Part of "The Cutter's Practical Guide to the Cutting and Making every kind of Garment"; for while I have done my utmost to make the work as complete as possible, so as to be of the greatest service to the cutter in daily practice, the publishers have brought it out in a style and finish which not only maintains their reputation, but excels, I think, any previous effort.

It has been my aim to place before my fellow craftsmen illustrations, diagrams, and descriptive letterpress of current styles, with the safest and best systems (according to my judgment) of the present day for producing them. In doing so, I have had very material help from some of the best specialist cutters in London; so that the special garments introduced in this work must be of great service to the cutter, as these give more trouble than the everyday class of orders.

It will be noticed I have made a few alterations in the Trouser System, chiefly to simplify and, if possible, make it plainer, and thus in my opinion improve it, although the principles are the same as in the "Federation Prize Essay". Thus, it will be seen, my endeavour has been to produce a work of real practical utility — one which would be a genuine help to the cutter amidst the worries of a peculiar and trying profession. In doing so I have left controversial subjects almost, if not entirely, out of the work.

If in this I have succeeded, and so placed the means of self-help within the reach of many, who, struggling amidst doubt and anxiety, are all the more eagerly seeking for light in the study of their profession, I shall be amply rewarded.

THE AUTHOR.

PUBLISHER'S PREFACE

The confidence with which this work was first introduced has been well justified by the result — a very large edition having been disposed of. Very rarely, if ever, has a work so comprehensive been published in connection with the art of cutting. For though nominally a work on Juvenile Cutting, it embraces nearly every garment made by tailors. Besides systems for and treatises on Trousers and Veats, systems for Morning Coats and Dress Coats, it also deals with Military Garments, Liveries, and many other garments, all worked out by a system which has now become well nigh universally popular, a special feature of the work being its beautifully engraved illustrations and diagrams. We have had very many indications that the work is highly appreciated by all who have procured it, and many testimonies might be recorded if that were necessary. This Third Edition has been prepared in all its original completeness. With such a work in their possession neither the inexperienced student nor the cutter in full practice should feel any difficulty in producing any of the garments treated and illustrated in this work.

THE JOHN WILLIAMSON COMPANY, LIMITED.

PREVIOUSLY PRINTED BY THE JOHN WILLIAMSON COMPANY LIMITED,
93 & 94 DRURY LANE, LONDON, W.C.

https://www.becomeatailor.com

Cutter's Practical Guide

TO

CUTTING AND MAKING

JUVENILE GARMENTS

Juvenile and Youths' Clothing.

Tailors generally do not view this important branch of the profession with the most kindly feelings, as, owing to the keen competition brought to bear by the ready-made houses, the prices are necessarily kept low; so that whilst many people do not object to pay a good price for their own garments, yet anything approaching a correspondingly proportionate figure for the juveniles would be considered most exorbitant; so that it will be necessary for those who aspire to clothe the coming race to be very expert in the matter of economy in every detail, and by its means be able to produce garments at a reasonable figure, and at the same time yield a living profit. A large one should never be attempted, as the tailor is sufficiently handicapped by the log to allow of any liberty being taken with the price. Nevertheless, although the immediate profit may not be large, yet this branch is well worth the attention of every tailor desirous of building up a lasting connection; for, by carefully catering for the wants of the boys, they are likely to think of "their tailor" after the leading strings are cast aside, and they are in a position to order their own attire, so that, in addition to the large amount of trade to be done at a reasonable profit, there is a connection to be built up, which must prove very beneficial to the firms who give this branch their careful study.

The systems as laid down in this work have been arranged with a view to simplicity and accuracy, and may be relied upon to produce smart and clean-fitting garments for the majority, and at the same time admitting of that ease or "growing room" most parents are anxious to impress on your mind as a positive necessity when giving the order.

As the scope of the work is very wide it will be as well to view it more as a treatise on practical cutting, adapted to youths and juveniles, than as a pure and simple juvenile work; accordingly we shall endeavour to explain such principles as will stand the test of meeting the vastly different wants of all the seven ages of man. It has been frequently pointed out that a knowledge of anatomy and mathematics is of very great service to the cutter, and as we shall endeavour to show every phase of science or art that can be brought to bear on the development of our profession, these must occupy a prominent position. Accordingly, we will take a brief glance at

Anatomy, Figures 1 and 2,

And its practical use to the tailor, in helping him to fashion a fitting covering for the image of God. It is not our intention to describe the formation of the skeleton in detail, but rather to point out such truths as will be of service to us as tailors, and foremost amongst these comes the fact that there are certain portions of the skeleton or framework which always remain near the surface; that is, in a thin man the bones may be felt very plainly at these places, and, no matter how fat the person may become, these particular parts are still only covered by a comparatively very thin portion of skin, as compared with other parts of the body. These parts are all marked with a cross on

Figures 1 and 2.

They are as follows: — 1. The shoulder joint, where the top of arm bone, collar bone and shoulder blade meet; 2. Each side of the elbow; 3. Each side of the wrist; 4. The spine, from top to bottom; 5. The hip bone; 6. The top of thigh bone, or hip joint; 7. The joint of knee; 8. The knee cap; 9. The shin bone, and others which are not necessary for the tailor to deal with. These will prove of great interest to the student, showing him that whatever the size of the individual these parts remain the same, and that when one part of the body is not in proportion to the other part the allowance must not be made at those parts where the bones come so near the surface as in the above instances, and consequently form the best starting points on which to base a system.

The inner dotted lines on these figures show the amount of muscle, in addition to which there is a thin layer of fat as well as the skin. Before we leave this subject there are one or two points worthy of our attention and study in

The Joints and their Movements,

as a knowledge of their actions enables us to know the possible from the impossible. A joint is formed by the junction of two bones, the extremities of which are perfectly adapted to each other, and every perfect joint consists of five parts, each of which has its function to perform. It is not our intention to treat with each part separately, as such would be beyond the application of anatomy to tailoring, but when we have to deal with the various kinds of joints, we have a subject which is of great interest to the tailor. There are

Three kinds of perfect joints.

The gliding joints which twist upon each other; they are composed of small, square bones, forming arches, the simplest form of which is found in eels and snakes; they are found in the back bone, the arch of the foot and the wrist. The next is the hinge, or swing joint, which moves to and fro, but has no side movement, the simplest illustration of which is the hinge of a door which moves only two ways, to and fro, swinging; these are usually the second and third joints of each member, thus, the second and third joints of the leg would be the knee and ankle; the second of the arm is the elbow; the second and third knuckles of the fingers and toes. If, for the sake of illustration you try the second joint of the finger, you will find it can only bend backwards and forwards; there is no sideways bend from the knuckle; all movements of that kind must come from the first joint, which leads us to the third kind of joint, viz., the ball and socket, or universal joint, which permits of great freedom of movement, in fact, moving all ways. They are mostly found at the commencement of a member, as at the shoulder, which is the freest of all joints; the hip joint, which is

slightly limited or restricted in some of its movements; the wrist, which is a complication of the ball and socket and gliding joints; the knuckles at the roots of the fingers, which enable the fingers to spread out; the roots of the toes, &c. If the reader will experiment with the various members of his own body he will readily fix this in his memory, As an illustration of the use of a knowledge of the movements of the various joints, we may take that of a figure on horseback; it is a common belief that the knee bends inwards, so as to cling to the horse, hence many systems have the centre line shifted 1, 1½, or 2 inches further from the front of fly line to produce this style of trousers; now, a knowledge such as we are treating of shows such a movement to be impossible; the outward movement, to allow of the horse being between the legs, comes from the hip joint, which is of the ball and socket kind, whilst the only movement the knee is capable of is the same as an ordinary hinge; hence, it will be seen the correct way to open the legs of a pair of trousers to make them follow the figure is to alter the angle at which the legs join the body, still letting the centre line start from the same spot. By this method the legs are kept straight, and the feet are made much more open than the knees, which has been proved by practical experience to be correct. These are some of the practical lessons to be obtained from a study of the human anatomy; they are, we think, very important ones, and should be remembered, as they help us very materially in dealing with special garments and abnormalities such as the

Corpulent Type of Figure,

Which, although vastly increased in size, yet has only the smallest amount at the sides and back, fully two-thirds, or even more of the corpulency going on the front. Boys very frequently partake of this build, especially the juveniles, but this will be readily gathered from the following table, which shows

The Development of Growth,

From 2½ years of age to 20, and which has been compiled and tested in the course of our practical experience at the cutting board. It has been arranged in accordance with the average age of a given size and height, which will, we have no doubt, be helpful to the trade generally, as it often happens that the cutter has to execute his orders from the most meagre measures which have been taken by parents, and which are frequently more misleading than otherwise.

Scale of Proportionate Measures.

Chest	Waist	Seat	Scye Depth	Nat. Waist	X Back	Sleeve	X Chest	Front Shoulder	Over Shoulder	Length of Vest	Leg	Height	Age
21	22	22	5½	9½	4½	16	4½	8¾	11⅜	15	13½	3ft.	2½
22	23	23	5¾	10¼	4¾	17½	4¾	9	11¾	15⅝	15	3ft. 3	3
23	23½	24	6	11	5	18	5	9¼	12¼	16¼	16½	3ft. 6	3½
24	24	25	6¼	11¾	5⅛	19½	5¼	9½	12¾	17	18	3ft. 9	4
25	24½	26	6½	12½	5⅜	21	5½	9¾	13¼	17½	19½	4ft.	5
26	25	27	6¾	13	5½	22½	5¾	10	13⅝	18¼	21	4ft.3	6
27	25½	28	7	13½	5¾	23¾	6	10¼	14	19	22½	4ft. 5	8
28	26	29	7¼	14	5⅞	25	6¼	10½	14¼	19½	24	4ft. 7	10
29	26½	30	7½	14½	6	26¼	6½	10¾	14½	20¼	25½	4ft. 9	11
30	27	31	7¾	15	6⅛	27½	6¾	11	14¾	21	27	4ft. 11	12
31	27½	32	8	15½	6⅜	28½	7	11¼	15⅛	21¾	28½	5ft. 1	13½
32	28	33	8¼	16	6½	29½	7⅛	11½	15½	22½	30	5ft 3	15
33	29	34	8½	16	6¾	30	7¼	11¾	15⅞	23	30¾	5ft. 5	16½
34	30	35	8⅝	16½	6⅞	31	7⅝	12	16¼	23½	30½	5ft. 7	18
35	31	36	8⅞	16½	7	31½	7¾	12¼	16⅝	24	32	5ft. 7½	19
36	32	37	9	17	7⅛	32	8	12½	17	24½	32½	5ft. 8	20

That this scale will be useful we have no doubt, and by working from it much better results can be obtained than by any divisions of the breast measure, for it is based on what has long been an acknowledged fact, that at birth the head is nearly one-fourth the total height of body, whilst at 7 or 8 it bears the relation of one-seventh, and at 16 it bears the same relative proportion as in the adult, which is differently computed at from 1 to 7½ to 1 to 8. A careful examination of this scale will also show how short the legs are in childhood as compared with the relations they bear as the child grows into the youth and the youth to the man.

It will also be noticed that between the ages of 2 and 4 the child grows in height very rapidly, gaining 9 inches in height as compared with 2 in the chest, a rate which is much in advance of his development in after years, and it will be well if all who wish to make juvenile clothing a specialty carefully study this table, as it shows most accurately the development of growth, from the baby to the young man, and, although different physiologists give various results of their observations, yet we believe such divergencies as exist between their tables may be traced to the varying conditions under which they were taken; still, the table as given will be found correct for the average English youth.

Artists' Relative Proportions.

From the very earliest records of art and artists we find the figure has been divided by them into so many parts, and by careful observation and measurements taken on a large number they have worked out a series of relative proportions, which should be of service to the tailor in producing a model pattern. Consequently we take the following from one of the best works published on this subject, entitled "Anatomy for Artists," by Dr. Fau: —

Proportions of the Human Figure.

"THE HUMAN FIGURE is so wonderfully constructed that many parts agree with each other in measurement — *e.g.*, the head and span, hand and face, nose and thumb, &c.; thus it is possible to use various parts in measuring the figure. In this table of proportions the unit is the head."

"FOR THE FIGURE. — When standing erect, the complete figure measures seven to seven and a half heads. When raised upon the toes, the height is eight heads; the latter is the more practical, from its giving the complete length of leg, and is easily divided — *e.g.*, take a line rather longer than desired length of figure; halve and quarter it; then halve the quarters into eighths of the line; this gives full length of the figure. For standing position, remove half of the lowest eighth, then the points of a figure seven and a half heads will be found. These are about the same in both sexes."

"THE HUMAN FIGURE IS SYMMETRICAL, THE HALVES BEING REVERSED. The pubic bone is the centre of the figure. The stretched-out arms give the height, the half is from pit of neck to tip of fingers, and is the same as from pubic bone to tip of toes. Thus we have three equal divisions of four heads in length."

4 HEADS IN LENGTH	(a) Pit of neck, to tip of fingers. (b) Top of head, to pubic bone. (c) Pubic bone, to toes.
2 HEADS LONG, OR ¼ OF FIGURE	1. Head, to nipples. 2. Nipples, to end of trunk. 3. End of trunk, to bump of tibia. 4. Bump of tibia, to extended toes. 5. Width of shoulders.

DISTANCES OF ABOUT 1½ HEAD IN LENGTH

Top of shoulder to elbow.
Elbow, to first knuckle.
Pit of neck, to navel.
From bottom of pectoral, to base of abdomen.
From base of abdomen to top of knee.
From bump of tibia, to top of instep.
Width of chest under armpits.
Width across thighs at trocanters.
From acromion process, to acromion process.

1 HEAD or 8TH OF LENGHT -

DISTANCES OF 1 HEAD

Top of head, to chin.
Chin, to nipples.
Nipples, to navel.
Navel, to base of pubic bone.
Base of pubic bone, to middle of thigh.
Middle of thigh, to bump of tibia.
Bump of tibia, to bottom of soleus.
Bottom of soleus, to tip of toes.
Between nipples, hollows of clavicles, and spines of ilium.
And length of buttock.

½ HEAD — Neck, knee, &c.

A reference to figure 2 A will show the relation the head bears to the other parts of the body in the average well-made figure, as above referred to, and which will be readily gathered is 7½ heads makes up the total height, the 8 heads theory being only correct in a very small number of cases, and when the person is very tall, in which case it will generally be found the legs are long in relation to the other parts. The Venuses and Apollos are generally looked upon as the highest ideals of proportion sculptors have ever produced, they are the statues that for ages have charmed the world, and have been looked upon as masterpieces of art; these all fall short of 8 heads, varying from 7¼ to 7¾ heads; consequently there can be little doubt that 7½ times the length of the head is the truest proportion. Vitruvius describes proportion as the equal measurement of the various constituent parts, in the existence of which symmetry is found to consist. Thus the distance from the tip of the finger to the tip of the finger, when the arms are outstretched, equals the height, and so on.

Now, although a knowledge of these relative proportions are of great service both to the artist and the tailor, it has long since been an acknowledged fact that they must not be relied on too implicitly; for example, in measurements taken by one of our best artists, with a view to test the accuracy of "the length of extended arms equals the height theory", it was found that out of 84 persons measured, 54 were found to be long-armed, 24 short-armed, and six only whose extended arms exactly equalled the total height. The greatest excess was in the case of a carpenter, whose arms exceeded his height by 5 inches, whilst the other extreme was an architect whose arms were 4 inches shorter than his height. Thus it will be seen these divisions must not be relied upon too implicitly, for

The Art of the Tailor

Consists more in dealing with abnormalities, and bringing them as nearly in appearance to these ideals of proportion; hence it is not only necessary for us to know what constitutes a proportionate figure, but also by the measures we take and the peculiarities of form we notice, to be able to detect wherein each customer varies from proportion, and by thus toning down the abnormalities to produce the most suitable garments for each customer. It is such work that transforms the science of tailoring to an art, and if we wish to rank as artist tailors and rise in our noble profession, those are the lines on which we must act and not use one pattern indiscriminately for all of a given size, and so produce the same style of garment, irrespective of the customer's peculiarities. It may be urged the pressure of business will not allow sufficient time for this, which is doubtless true in many cases, but if we aspire to reach the top of the ladder of fame it is the only way it can be attained, and as there is always plenty of room in the upper stories of our profession for really good men, whilst the lower branches are always too crowded, we can only exhort our readers to aim high, and, by diligent application and study, master every problem connected with our calling, and make themselves worthy of the highest position the trade can offer.

This, we think, will be sufficient of anatomy to fully explain all there is to be learnt in connection with it and tailoring, so we will now turn our attention to another science, viz.,

Geometry,

Or that branch of mathematics which investigates the relations, properties and measurements of solids, surfaces, lines, and angles; consequently, any system of cutting is, strictly speaking, a development of geometry, for the whole thing is arranged by taking certain measures of the body, and, by the aid of lines, curves, and angles, to produce a pattern that shall be a fitting covering for the surface of the body. Taken, however, in the light in which it is generally viewed, there is one fact which must always be of use to the tailor in his daily practice, and that is to know the relation the diameter bears to the circumference of a true circle; this has been deduced to the following proportions, which, for all practical tailoring purposes, are sufficiently correct. It is as follows: — A trifle under a third, or in the relation of 7 to 22, or as 113 is to 355; of course, it is quite useless for us to go into fractions, $\frac{7}{22}$ is quite near enough for any use we may put it to, and means that if the circumference be divided in 22 equal parts, the diameter would be seven of those parts; this will be valuable knowledge in dealing with such sections as the neck, scye, &c.

The degrees at which the various angles are drawn need not be studied, as the tailor always has his square and chalk handy, which are quite sufficient to enable him to draw a line at any angle he may choose; in fact, it is so generally the custom of the trade to go down 9 and out 1, or down 12 and out 3, and so on, in order to produce an angle of any given degree, that we should only be adding mystery to a very simple matter, and from which no compensating improvement would accrue, and as such is not our intention, it being rather our aim to simplify simplicity than to produce a complicated work of use only to the few.

There is one other geometrical fact worth our noting as being of use to the cutter; viz., that all points of a circle are the same distance from its centre, so that if we wish to draw a part of a circle by sweeping it will be the same distance at all points from the centre; these are the practical lessons of geometry and anatomy. Not much, you will say! still, of great value in daily practice, and we especially commend them to the careful consideration of the reader.

Art.

So much might be said on this topic that we feel we should be overlooking a most important factor in successful cutting if we did not make some allusion to it, for not only must we have the seams to run in graceful curves and devoid of all sharp angles, &c., but they must be also arranged

so as to bring out the special points of beauty which exists in a more or less degree in every figure, as well as toning down other prominent points which detract from its graceful appearance. As regards the production of harmony and grace in outline, we do not know of anything better to illustrate how this principle is applied than

Hogarth's Line of Beauty,

And which may be advantageously introduced to the outline of almost every garment at some part or other, and certainly the principle involved in it is most valuable, as it teems with grace at every part. This is illustrated on plate 24, and it will astonish the student to see how often it recurs in almost every graceful object. Then, again, the question of colour must always occupy an important place in the consideration of every cutter, and may be briefly stated, as all those colours which attract the light, such as white, &c., apparently increase the size of the figure, whilst all dark ones such as black, &c., have the opposite effect. Patterns of the material also have a great effect; stripes add to the height or width of the figure wearing them, according to the direction in which they run; thus, a stripe running up and down the figure adds to the height, whilst one with the stripes running across has the opposite effect, viz., of adding to the width and detracting from the height, an effect which is anything but desirable. Large checks add to the size of the figure without adding to the height, and are not generally considered suitable for youths. We shall, however, return to this subject again, so we will pass on.

The principles of cutting coats are fully explained by us in Part 2 of "The Cutter's Practical Guide to the Cutting Board" which treats of all kinds of Body Coats, and as vests are similar to coats it would be superfluous for us to go over them again; trousers also having been treated of fully in the "National Work on Trouser Cutting", Vol. I., we will at once proceed to consider the method of

Taking the Measures.

This should always be done carefully and methodically, for however good a system may be, if the measures are not taken correctly it is a moral impossibility for the garments cut by them to fit, so that too much care cannot be taken in this direction. It should also be borne in mind that most parents desire their children's garments to fit them easily, yet, at the same time, to hang gracefully, and it has always been our custom to find out at the time of measuring the degree of ease desired; it being comparatively easy at this stage to gather your customer's views in this direction, which often vary considerably.

The measures we advise to be taken are as follows:

FOR COATS.

1. The depth of scye at back, which may be obtained as follows: Place the tape over the shoulders, saddle fashion, down in front of both arms, and back under the arms close up to the armpit till they meet in the centre of back, as shown on figures 3 and 4, at which point make a mark with a piece of pipe clay, as at B, figure 4, care being taken to see that the tape, in crossing the back, runs neither up nor down, keeping it as nearly as possible level, taking the floor as a guide; measure to be taken from A to B.

2. Length from collar seam to natural waist.

3. Length from collar seam to full length desired.

4. Width across back, with the arm resting at the side, as if taken with the arm raised, it makes the back too wide. Now

lift the arm up, carry it well forward, and give it a decided bend at the elbow, after which continue the measure on from

5. Centre of back to elbow.

6. Centre of back to hand.

7. Now take the width across chest from the front of right scye to front of left scye, E to E, figure 3.

8. Length of front shoulder, from collar seam at back to bottom of scye in front, which may be easily obtained by placing the finger under the arm, from A to D.

9. From mark made at depth of scye at B, over the shoulder at C, and down in front of arm to the level of scye in front at D. This is the over shoulder measure.

10. Size of chest taken fairly close.

11. Size of waist taken in the same manner.

12. Size of seat taken in the same manner. Measures 10 and 11 should be taken *over the vest only* for all kinds of garments, variations being easily made for different styles.

FOR VESTS.

13. Length from nape of neck to opening required (not to the top button).

14. Continued on to full length, and where ño jacket is ordered it will be necessary to take the size of chest, waist, and the four direct measures, 1, 7, 8, 9, those published in the scale, page 3, may be used when the customer is fairly proportionate.

FOR TROUSERS.

15. The full length of side.
16. The full length of leg.
17. The size of waist.
18. The size of seat.
19. The size of thigh, (tight), both dress and undress sides.
20. The size of knee, fashion width.
21. The size of bottom.

FOR BREECHES.

22. The length of side, from top to knee.
23. The length to knee from crutch.
24. The length of small.
25. The length of calf bottom, &c., from crutch.
26. Size of waist.
27. Size of seat.
28. Size of thigh, (tight) dress and undress sides.
29. Size of knee.
30. Size of small.
31. Size of calf and bottom.

FOR SHIRT.

32. Size of neck.
33. Size of chest.
34. Size of waist.
35. Length of sleeve.
36. Length of body required.

When they will probably stand in the order book as follows: every detail likely to be of service to you being obtained from the customer at the time of measuring and entered in the order book: —

S.B. Lounge, 2 x flaps, ticket flaps, 1 out b. left, 1 in b. right, 7, 15, 23, 5⅝, 17, 27½, 6¾, 11, 14¾, 30, 27, 31.

Step collar Vest, W.P., guard hole 2 and 3, 9, 21.

F.F., side pockets.

37, 27, 26, 31, 18, 19½, 16, 16.

Breeches, F.F., x pockets, seat strapped and lined chamois, 22, 12, 14, 16½, 26, 31, 18, 19¼, 11½, 10, 11½.

Shirt. — 13½, 30 27, 27, 27½, 31.

As will be seen these measures are much the same as those usually taken, the principal addition being Nos. 1, 7, 8 and 9, and which come under the heading of DIRECT MEASURES, and despite the idea that many people have of being able to take these correctly, we fail to see the difficulty, as the way suggested is at once both simple and effective, and as the best of systems will produce but poor results in the hands of indifferent workmen, this will prove no exception with them, but in the hands of an intelligent tailor we are positive of the success of the method, far beyond any plain and simple breast measure plan. The purpose for which these extra measures are taken are as follows: No. 1 and 8, find the depth of scye and fix the balance in accordance with the requirements of the figure; No. 7 is to locate the scye in its proper position in relation to the front and back, and No. 9 is used to ascertain the height of shoulder or what is perhaps better known as the shoulder slope. Every one of these measures can be applied direct to the draught and as they are taken over the garment it will *not* be necessary to allow anything for seams.

In such garments as fasten up to the neck it would be advisable to supplement these measures with the size of neck and the height of front, which may be fixed as follows: place the tape at collar seam behind and measure down the front to any point fancy may dictate, say 12, and having noted this quantity keep the tape fixed at this latter point 12, release it from the back and bring the tape up to the front of neck which measures applied direct will effectually find the height of neck in front. Having thus carefully considered the various measures and the qualities possessed by each we will pass on to give the proportion they usually bear to the breast measure in a person whose height agrees with and is in general proportion to his chest measure.

In the majority of figures these four measures bear a RELATION TO THE BREAST measure as follows:

The depth of scye, one-fourth.

The front shoulder, ½ inch more than ⅓

The cross chest, 1 inch less than ¼.

And the over shoulder, 1 inch less than half.

Another Way of Proving these

Is to take ⅓ scye and ⅙ natural waist for the scye depth, the front shoulder at this quantity plus one-twelfth breast and ½ an inch, the over shoulder by adding these two together and deducting 1½ times the shoulder slope previously fixed by ⅙ of the natural waist, and the across chest measure in the same way as above, for example, a 36 breast with natural waist at 18 and scye at 18 would be as follows: ⅓ scye and ⅙ natural waist equals 9, this quantity plus one-twelfth breast and ½ inch 12½. These two added together equal 21½ less 1½ times shoulder slope 4½ equal. 17, across chest 1 inch less than ¼ equal 8, so that these four measures can be calculated in this manner if no opportunity occurs for measuring and the scale is not at hand. In such a case however it is better to have a set of block patterns to use from, drafted out to the measures in this scale which will be found quite reliable and better than calculated divisions of the breast, as it is a generally recognized fact that various breast measures have different characteristics, each of which has been specially treated of in this scale.

THE SYSTEM

FOR PRODUCING THE VARIOUS GARMENTS.

We do not think we could begin on any more appropriate garment than

The Shirt. Dias. 1, 2, 3, 4, 5, 6. Fig. 5.

Begin by drawing line 0, 36, and mark off the length desired. Make 0 to 2½, ⅙ neck and continue across to 9, ½ breast; come down from 0 to 2 ¼, ⅛ natural waist to find top of shoulder, and draw a line across to top, and shape shoulder from 2½ to 9. 0 to 3; ½ an inch more than ⅙ neck and draw the gorge as shown from points 3 to 2½ keeping it hollow as illustrated, or if a guide is wanted, draw a line from 2½ to 3 and midway between these two points hollow it ¾ of an inch. 0 to 9 is ¼ breast, draw a line across to 11½ making it a ¼ breast and 2½ inches for a moderately close-fitting shirt or 3 inches for a looser style, hollow scye by coming in 1 in. from line at 9 as at point 1, and shape side seam to taste or fancy, allow 2 inches all down either side of the front to avoid having a seam at the pleats for buttonholes and button stand, or if a white shirt is desired cut it to allow of a front being inserted as per dotted line, which may be varied to taste.

The Yoke. Diagram 2,

Is cut by the front; raising the back neck half the distance from 0 to 3, and cutting it a ½ inch wider at scye as per diagram, the back part should be cut on the crease or seams allowed, otherwise the neck will be too small. The bottom of yoke may be shaped to taste.

The back is also cut from the front taking it across straight from the shoulder point and leaving a good 2½ inches down centre of back to be gathered or pleated in to the yoke, the scye should be filled in a good inch and the bottom made about 2 inches longer than the front.

The Sleeve.

Draw line 0, 9, 0, 17; 0 to 2½ is the same as the distance from 9 to 11½ of the forepart, 0 to 9 is the half scye plus whatever is desired to be left for fulness or pleats on the shoulders; 2½ to 17 is the length of sleeve less the width of yoke and length of cuff; and the wrist as at 17, 6 to taste varying according to the fulness desired to be put into the wristband. Both parts of the sleeves are cut alike, that part at 2½, 17 being cut on the crease, and in putting it into the armhole point 9 goes to 11½ of the forepart being just at the underarm seam.

The cuff, Dia. 5, may be reproduced either by the inch tape for the 36 size or graduated tapes for the smaller sizes. The collar, Dia. 6, is an ordinary band and is cut on the lines of a stand collar; draw line 0, 15 the length of neck plus 1 inch to allow of it buttoning, 0 to 7½ half this quantity, come up at either end 1 inch, and shape the bottom edge by a gradual curve touching the line for about 2 or 3 inches on either side of point 7½ finish by making the width of the band to any width desired. Binders are sometimes put round the armholes, being cut the same shape as the shirt at that part and are merely put on to strengthen the shirt there, and relieve it of some of, the wear.

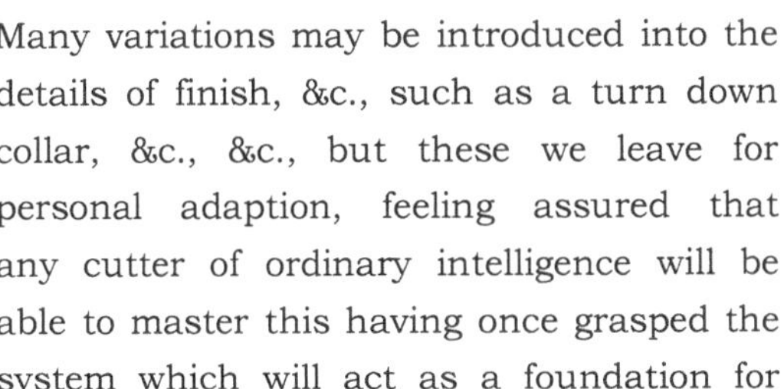

Many variations may be introduced into the details of finish, &c., such as a turn down collar, &c., &c., but these we leave for personal adaption, feeling assured that any cutter of ordinary intelligence will be able to master this having once grasped the system which will act as a foundation for him to start from.

We now come to one of the most important parts in connection with the work, viz.:

THE LOUNGE SYSTEM.
Diagram 7. Figs. 6 & 7.

Commence by drawing line 0, 29 and mark off the various stations on it as follows: 0 to 9 depth of scye, 0 to 17 natural waist, 0 to 29 length of jacket required plus ½ inch for seams, point 3½ is fixed to taste, but as a rule may be made about ½ inch more than ⅓ of 0, 9; draw lines at right angles to all these points and mark off 0 to 3 ⅙ neck; or if the neck measure has not been taken, make it ⅙ of the half waist; at the back pitch which is about 1 or 1½ below line 3½ mark off the width of back plus seams. In the scale the seams are allowed on the back so that when working from it, it will not be necessary to allow them beyond the quantities given, but when working from the measures taken on the customers this must be done or the back will be produced narrower than was anticipated. Hollow the back at waist ⅜ to ½ inch, running out to the line at bottom; on line at 9, mark off the chest measure and from 2 to 2½ inches, varying this quantity according to the substance of the material, allowing the full 2½ inches over breast; if the material is thick or if it is of medium weight allow 2 inches; of this about 1½ inches are consumed in seams, the remainder being an amount of room left for expansion of the body when breathing, &c., and for ease.

Now come back from 20 to 12 the across chest measure which finds the front of scye.

The Neck Point.

Deduct the width of back neck from the front shoulder measure, and sweep by it from point 12; add 1 inch to this and sweep again by point 20, and wherever these arcs intersect or cross each other fixes the location of the neck point.

The over-shoulder measure is the next to be applied, the method of doing so being to deduct whatever the back measures from 9 in a diagonal measure to the shoulder seam, put the remainder at point 12; put the finger on the tape 1½ inches up and sweep again, this gives the slope of shoulder, and it only remains to draw the shoulder seam by well rounding it and making the width to agree with a seam less than the back from ¾ to 7¼.

Having now practically fixed the top, bottom, front, and back, of scye, we only have to connect the various points; the shape of a scye should as nearly resemble the shape of a horseshoe as possible, though if special attention is paid to any particular part it should be to make the front well hollow at * and keep it well up at the top of sideseam. Some may feel curious to know the reason we place the finger 1½ inches up from the level of scye and sweeping from * in applying the over shoulder measure. The reason for doing so is, that we always endeavour to apply. the measures in the same way as they are taken, which would not be the case if a sweep was taken from point 12, the tape would then cross the scye, a feature quite impossible in taking the measure on the figure.

The shaping of the sideseam is the next operation, and is one which has much to do with the harmony of the jacket when

finished; the plan illustrated here is to fix the width of back at natural waist at ⅓ chest; *i.e.*, the half chest, and taking out from 1 to 1½ inches at that part, seldom more than that as it is apt to throw a fulness at top of sideseam; the back and forepart should touch each other on line 9, 20, and a trifle may be taken out just above where it runs into the back scye; avoid letting the forepart come too high up into the back scye, from 1 to 1½ inches above depth of scye line is a very good quantity, as it prevents the possibility of balance being altered by the workman, which might soon occur if the back scye ran up to a point. The forepart is made to overlap the back ½ the difference between the seat and breast measures at the bottom of the sideseam. If the waist is desired to fit close at the sides and a smart fitting garment required we should take out a fish under the arm, running from the bottom of scye to the pocket mouth, of from ½ to 1 inch and making the size up in front to the waist measure and 2 inches, which gives the breast line or that part of the garment which runs down the centre of the figure and which would be correct for hooks and eyes; lounges however are usually made to fasten with buttons so that it will be necessary to allow sufficient overlap, say 1¼ inches. The height of the gorge at front may be made ⅙ neck or breast, below the neck point, or to taste; and the front of jacket should be ¾ of an inch longer from line 9, 20, downwards than the back and rounded off to any style desired.

The Position of the Pockets

Is a matter which puzzles a good many, and the plan we have found to answer well has been to make the hip pocket ⅓ breast from the bottom of scye, and making the flap ½ this distance in length and from 1¾ to

2 inches wide, shaping the front to harmonize with the front of the jacket, the ticket pocket may be placed parallel with it in front and about in the relative position to the hip pocket as shown on the diagram. The breast pocket should be placed level with the bottom of the scye for its bottom edge it is made to slant slightly down and kept at least 1 inch in front of the scye the size of this being 5 inches long by 1 in width for a 36 chest and in corresponding ratio for smaller ones. The buttons down the front should be arranged, so that the bottom one comes just above the level of the hip pockets, and if possible it should be arranged to have one opposite the breast pocket.

The Sleeve. Dia. 9.

That the sleeve should be cut to fit the scye is an almost self-evident truism; yet it is one that is often ignored, with the result that they do not harmonize with each other and bad fitting sleeves are the consequence.

The sleeve system as here described is as self-varying as any system can be and one which will produce a nice hanging sleeve. Begin by drawing line 0, 1, 4¾; from 0 to 4¾ is the distance from centre of back to front of scye less the width of the back, in this case 4¾; now mark the place where the pitches of the sleeve are desired to come; suitable positions for these are ¾ above level of scye in front and about 1½ below shoulder point of back. Now put the square with either arm touching these pitches, and arrange it till it is in the position in which the sleeves are desired to hang which should be as nearly as possible over the pockets, note what figures are on the square opposite the front pitch and apply this quantity by coming up from point 4¾ of sleeve whatever it is, and thus find the position of point 1; now measure the distance across between the two pitches in a straight line, with the back placed in a closing position at the shoulder, and whatever that is, measure across as from 1 to 9; point 4½ is half this quantity, and 2¼ one fourth and by these points the sleeve head may be drawn; measure off the length to elbow and wrist, not forgetting that 3 seams are consumed in making up; hollow the forearm 1 inch and make the width to taste which in the absence of any better guide may be fixed at ⅓ breast for the cuff and 1 inch less than half breast for the elbow; the run of the bottom of cuff may be got by drawing it at right angles to points 6¼, 9. The underside is got by measuring round the scye between the two pitches and applying that quantity from 4¾ to 8, hollowing it about ½ an inch below a level with 4¾, and then taking it across almost straight.

This style of garment is one of the most suitable for boys' and youths' wear, being particularly appropriate for school use. It is usually made up as represented having 5 pockets, as shown on diagram, and an inside breast pocket. It is made to button fairly high up, the edges stitched and the cuff also stitched to form a cuff, two buttons being put on as shown.

To Reproduce by Graduated Tapes.

This and any diagram in the book may be reproduced by using a graduated tape to agree with the breast measures and applying the units in the same way as the inches are for the full size; if of the old make using a tape a size larger for the small sizes and a size smaller for the very large ones, say a 12½ tape for a 24, and a 21½ for a 44 and so on; or they may be drawn out by the scale given previously by merely using the ordinary inch tape in the manner described. This system is the same as goes throughout the book so that if the reader makes himself conversant with the principles on which this is based, he will be more readily able to reproduce any garment in the present volume, by merely varying it in accordance with the lines laid down in dealing with each garment. We give the collar system later on. Although this diagram is illustrated with a collar and turn yet it is equally suitable for a Prussian, roll, or stand collar, only requiring the collar cut to suit the customers' wishes in that direction. Care should be taken in making to avoid anything likely to produce fulness at the top of sideseam as owing to the placing of the seams in this style of jacket there is a difficulty in providing a sufficient receptacle for the blades and a corresponding tendency to fulness at top of sideseam, hence it is just as well to take it in a trifle just at the top and put the sleeve in tight at that part. A short collar should be religiously avoided as besides having a tendency to produce this defect, it is also a fruitful source of many others to be frequently met with in all classes of coats; but we shall refer to them in our chapter on alterations, &c., so will at once proceed to examine the characteristics of the

D.B. REEFER.
Dia. 8. Fig. 8.

At the present time this is one of the most fashionable styles, and is especially suitable for youths' wear, leaving full scope for putting the buttons forward as the lad grows, a point which often has great weight with the parents. This garment is also used a good deal in H. M. Navy, being worn by almost all ranks and especially by Midshipmen and Cadets; they however generally omit the ticket pocket and have gilt anchor buttons, 4 up each front, one being placed under the turn; three are placed across the cuff as dia. 10, which are the same size as those up the front. As will be noticed it is cut precisely the same as the Lounge with the addition of the lapel all down the front from 2½ to 3½ inches wide. In this case it is made 3, the buttons being placed as far behind the breast line as the eye of the hole is in front, a fish is taken out at the top of lapel which will enable it to button up to the throat clean, this may be omitted if desired the only difference being a little extra length on the outside edge. The collar and lapel as shown on this dia. illustrates the style in which these are finished at the present time, very little space showing between them. If it is desired to make this garment from a thick pilot or nap we should advise the size being made at least ½ an inch or more larger and the cut under the arm omitted, as these thick materials consume a great deal in making, and being of a heavier substance do not fall in wrinkles as readily as a thin estamene or serge.

The pockets are arranged as for the lounge.

THE NORFOLK JACKET.
Dia. 11. Fig. 9.

No style of garment of a fancy kind has remained so long in favour as this, and it is worn by boys, youths, and men, in almost the same style; a great variety exists as to the style of putting on the pleats, the most popular being the one shown on the diagram and having two up the back and front, meeting at the same spot on the shoulder. It is now the pretty universal custom to cut the garment as a Lounge, rather easy-fitting about the waist, and to lay the pleats on, fastening them to the garment by sewing them from behind, this has proved itself the most reliable and artistic method as it enables the cutter to arrange the pleats on the figure, in whatever position may be considered the most suitable and at the same time removing any possibility of the garment being made larger or smaller by the workmen in making, an error which readily happens when the foreparts are cut wide enough for the pleats to be taken from them. The most reliable method of forming

The Pleats

In this style is to have them sewn and pressed open previous to cutting the garment, which overcomes the difficulty. As will be noticed the pleat and belt are stitched on the edge in the same way as the edges are stitched, the pleats however are often left plain. The belt should be made the same size as the garment and a button put further back to allow of its being made smaller. The belt and pleat, Dia. 12, are usually made to agree in widths and are about 1¾ or 2 inches wide for a 36 breast and of proportionate width for the smaller sizes. The pockets on this style of garment are either placed under the pleat at breast or patch as shown on diagram 11, and an in breast pocket in the ordinary position. Variations innumerable are introduced in the method of arranging the pleats for the juvenile branch, but this we shall notice later on, under the heading of designing but there is one style which is a good deal used for youths and men, which only has one pleat up the back and one down each front, running into the gorge, this style is generally finished with a Prussian collar, but of course any style of collar and turn may be used. The sleeve as shown on diagram 9, is equally suitable for this as for the Lounge.

THE INFANTRY PATROL JACKET.
Diagrams 13 and 14. Figure 10.

The Patrol Jacket forms quite a distinct class of garment, being a much smarter and closer-fitting garment than the ordinary

Lounge, and we thought it could not be better illustrated than by trimming it in one of the most popular styles in vogue in the British Army, viz., the Infantry Blue Patrol Jacket. The Patrol Jacket was worn very much at one time by cyclists, though the Lounge is the most popular for this exercise at present. The official regulations for such, as issued by the War Office, are as follows: "Bottom corners rounded, slit at side, stand collar, hook and eyes down front, flat braided all round with 1 inch wide mohair braid, four drop loops of ⅜ wide tubular braid, the top one 8 inches long, the bottom one-six, to the edge of breast, with an eye at the centre as in diagram 13, on the left side the braid is carried a loop beyond the edge and olivets or barrel buttons on the right side; sideseam braided as shown, the middle of crow's toe at bottom to be 3 inches from the centre of back, and the middle of the braid at the lowest of the middle eyes 2 inches, the top crow's toe to be at the top of sideseam; a plain Austrian knot is placed on the sleeve seven inches high and two and three-quarters wide, and placed rather nearer the forearm seam; jetted cross pockets, with flaps to go in or out."

Such being the military regulations, it will at once be seen that the Patrol Jacket proper is more of a military that a civilian type of garment, consequently its shape must be influenced by it, and the following variations will be found necessary or advisable. The back being cut whole, i.e., no back seam, it necessarily follows the back must be straight, hence line O, 28½ forms the centre of back. The shoulder seam of back is kept rather squarer, which will bring that of the forepart more sloping. The back is cut 2 inches wide at the natural waist, point 17, and 3 inches wide at the bottom, so that the braiding may come just over the seam. 1½ inches is taken out between back and sidebody at waist, and run into the depth of scye line, and also slightly overlapping say ¼ of an inch at the bottom, 1 inch is taken out of the underarm seam, and the chest made up to 2 or 2¼ over the chest measure, the waist being done in like manner. Care must be used so as not to cut the neck too low or the neck will be too large. The sleeve on diagram 9 is equally suitable. So that it will not be necessary for us to repeat instructions for cutting these.

The Austrian Knot,

However, is a bit of puzzle to many, and we herewith give diagrams, descriptions and directions for tying. The first thing is to cut off the necessary length of braid; a knot of the dimensions quoted from the Army Regulations for an Infantry Patrol Jacket can be completed with one yard which allows sufficient to go round top of sleeve and be joined in with the hind arm seam. Now take this length between the forefinger and thumb about six inches from the end, and form the loop as per diagram 15, then continue on with another loop, which brings back over the other and under the short length as per diagram 16. Great care must be used at this stage, as the whole secret lies in knowing when and whence to begin lacing. Now proceed to lace over and under alternately, as per diagram 17, and when this stage is completed, it will present the appearance of diagram 18, when all that remains to be done is to form the loop at the top, see diagram 19, which will necessitate a half twist through half the knot, which is best done at this stage, as it is very easy to twist the wrong way if done earlier. Carefully examine to see that the braid runs alternately over and under throughout the entire knot, and if formed correctly, which it will be if these directions are followed. When it is ready

to be put on, its position should be, as previously quoted: top of knot about 7 inches
from bottom of cuff; and as it is necessary
it should appear on the top of the sleeve, it
must be placed about one inch nearer the
forearm seam.

The Eton Jacket.

This is one of the most important styles
in connection with the present work, being
the garment above all others the high-class
tailor is called upon to make. It bears
very much the same relation to the youth
that the Dress Coat does to the man, being
worn on such occasions as demand full
dress, although in many of our public
schools it is always worn in every day wear.
It is seldom or ever worn buttoned, consequently it is not cut with too much bottom
stand, ¾ of an inch being quite enough at
the bottom, the lapel at the top being quite
a matter of taste, but should not be made
too heavy. The better plan is to cut a pattern and turn it over at the crease row, and
see that it does not come nearer the scye
than 1½ inches, as it looks very old-fashioned
to see a lapel coming right over the sleeve
head. As generally worn all over the
country, the Eton Jacket is made about 3½
inches below the natural waist and finished
off with a point at the bottom of the back,
as worn at Eton, however, the point is
omitted and carried straight round, which
makes it appear rather shorter. It is generally supposed that the Eton Boys wear
the white linen collar outside the coat, and
that the Harrow Boys wear it inside,
whether any regulations exist in this we do
not know, but believe such to be the fact.
The Eton plan, however, is the one more
generally adopted throughout the country,
and it will be as well to note that when it
is desired to wear the linen collar inside,
it will be necessary to enlarge the neck to
allow for this increase of size. However,

as we are catering for the youths all over
the country, we have given a diagram suitable for the style most generally adopted,
and which is illustrated on

Diagram 20. Plate 4. Figure 11.

As will be seen the back is cut on the
crease as in the Patrol Jacket, and is made
rather narrow at the waist being cut about
1¼ inches wide at that part, and gradually
run off to the bottom, which as previously
quoted is finished with a point; 1½ inches
is taken out between back and sidebody,
and about ¾ of an inch at the waist of
underarm seam. Care should be taken to
allow sufficient spring for the hips, a point
which sometimes causes trouble, especially.
as the inlay, which is invariably left all
along the bottom, contracts it. The length
of the front should be made to just cover
the vest in the same way as a Gent's Dress
Coat, nothing appearing much worse than
one too short, or one very much too long,
and conveying the appearance that the lad
is wearing out the jacket his older brother
has grown out of; the diagram is arranged
with the front cut as much below waist
seam as the bottom of sidebody is below
point 2¾, and will generally be found a safe
guide, and which will also be of service to
hollow the side by, this being made
about 1 inch hollow from a line drawn from
bottom of sidebody to the bottom of front.
The lapel on this diagram is made 1¾ inches
wide at top, 2¼ in the widest part, and ¾ at
the bottom; the gorge is lowered 1 inch in
front.

These jackets are generally made from a
fine black diagonal, a kind of dress Twill or
Corkscrew, have generally bound edges, the
binding is never carried round the bottom,
it being invariably left bluff, the inlay
being turned up all along at that part, so
that only the fronts, collars and cuffs are
bound. This make of cloth has entirely

superceded the old superfine black cloth which is hardly or ever seen. We have occasionally seen them made from Vicuna or soft wool, with corded edges, but these have been the exception. A good facing should be put through the forepart, and one or two in breast pockets inserted. A flower hole is sometimes put in the turn, but it is as often left plain. There are three button-holes only put up the front, as a rule, although we sometimes see four. The style of cuff generally adopted, is illustrated on

Diagram 25,

Which is nothing more than the ordinary hole and button cuff, with the braid put on cuff high, and brought to the end of the slit which it is just as well to very slightly round at the bottom which does away to a considerable extent with the tendency slit cuffs have to curl up at the points. In order to get this garment to fit to perfection, great care should be taken to get it to balance exactly to the figure, as if it is too long in the front it will set away from the waist at back and have a general "falling away from the figure" appearance, whilst if it is too short, it presents an all-alive appearance with any amount of surplus material on the back, hence it is always better to err in a too-long front shoulder than a too short one for this class of garment.

The Vest.
Diagram 59.

For this Jacket, is either of the no collar or roll collar type, and is of course finished in the same way, and made from the same material as the coat. For school wear, it is generally made no collar, but when worn for semi-dress occasions, of the roll collar, button rather high type, as diagram 61, and when for full dress, the present hollow cut front or horseshoe dress vest is used as in diagram 62, so that a fair amount of latitude is allowed with this part of the Eton suit.

The Trousers

Are invariably made from black for all dress and semi-dress wear; but for school wear they are frequently made from any dark neat pattern material such as West of England Hairline; it should, however, be remembered that the correct thing is black, and any variation from that must be particularly neat, only being permissible on account of its increased usefulness and wear resisting qualities for school use. One point to be especially remembered is, that the seat of these trousers shows very conspicuously, so that it is not allowable to put in seat pieces or take out cuts that will show below-the Jacket, as such would give a "short of material" impression. Care should also be taken in cutting these to avoid all surplus material, (only allowing 1½ over seat instead of 2 inches), and to get them to fit as clean as possible at the back of thighs, just under the ball of the seat. They must be much cleaner fitting at this part than ordinary trousers, so that if the seat angle is slightly reduced it will improve them so far as fit is concerned, though it will reduce the bending or stooping capacity somewhat. It is just such little details as these that are noticed by parents, and add materially to the success and renown of the tailor. The pockets of the trousers are put in across the top as the side style gape so much; but this is one of those points wherein it will be necessary to consult the wishes of your customer, it not being of very great importance which plan is adopted, though the cross, being much neater, are decidedly preferable.

It may be of service to our readers if we give a list of the articles usually required by youths about to go to any of the leading public schools and colleges.

1 Best Suit.	1 Football Suit.
2 School Suits.	4 Neck Ties.
1 Overcoat.	1 Neck Wrapper.
1 Dressing Gown.	1 Silk Hat.
8 White Shirts, or	1 Polo Cap.
6 Coloured Shirts, or	1 Rug.
4 Flannel Shirts.	1 Umbrella.
4 Night Shirts.	4 Towels.
4 Under Shirts.	2 Bath Towels.
4 pairs Drawers.	1 Sponge and Bag.
8 pairs Hose or Half Hose.	2 Combs & Brushes.
	1 Bag for ditto.
1 doz. Collars.	1 Tooth Brush.
1 doz. Handkerchiefs.	1 Nail Brush.
2 pairs Gloves.	1 Clothes Brush.
2 Braces.	1 pair Bathing Drawers.
2 Strong Lace Boots.	
	4 Dinner Napkins.
1 pair Calf Shoes.	Knife, Fork, and Spoon.
1 Patent Dress Shoes.	
	2 pairs Sheets.
1 Slippers.	4 Pillow Cases.
1 Leggings.	Trunk.
1 Leggings Athletic.	Play Box.
1 Boots or Shoes.	Leather Bag.
1 Cricketing Suit.	Key Ring and Label.

Varieties of the Eton Jacket.
Diagrams 21 and 22. Figures 12 and 13.

These are supposed to partake of the Naval Style of Dress. The Admirals Round Jacket being somewhat similar to the D.B. Eton, of Diagram 21; it is also used in the Merchant Service, it is, however, more a variation from the regulation Naval Dress, than a copy of any authorized pattern.

Its principal features are the increased width of the lapel, more especially at waist, and the two rows of buttons. All Naval Jackets for lads have pockets placed at the sides as shown on diagram 22, but these are always omitted from Civilian Dress, the pockets in the latter case being put in the breast. The badge on the collar is generally a matter of taste.

The Eton Jacket with Roll Collar

Comes as something new, and now that this style of front is so popular with gentlemen for their Dress Coats, we quite anticipate it becoming an established style of Youth's Dress, for evening wear, it being very smart and effective. It is also shown as a naval adaptation, having a badge on the collar and pockets at the side.

If these latter styles are desired for representations of naval uniform, the cuffs are as shown on diagram 26, which has three gilt uniform buttons, with cords of Russia Braid coming nearly to the bottom, whilst, if intended for ordinary Dress wear, that shown on Diagram 25, will be the better; at the same time remembering what was previously stated regarding the pockets.

We now come to deal with the naval uniforms proper for the Midshipmen and Cadet, illustrated on figures 14 and 15, and diagrams 23, 24, 26 and 27, and take first,

THE MIDSHIPMAN'S ROUND JACKET.

The official regulations for this are as follows: "Blue cloth, single-breasted, with nine holes and buttons up the front, three notched holes on each cuff with buttons to correspond; stand up collar, with a white turn back on each side 2 inches long, with a notched hole and button." It is cut exactly the same as an Eton Jaket in the back and the fronts arranged as Diagram 23 from which it will be readily gathered it is cut large enough to button right up to the throat. Care should be taken to put only the regulation number of buttons up the front, 9. Welt pockets are put on either side as shown. The only difference between this and the Cadets, is that the white turn back is omitted, and a button hole of white twist, and a uniform button placed instead. This applies to both the Round Jacket and

Which as will be seen is of the Dress Coat type, but made large enough to button; with 9 notched holes up the front, graduated as shown, the longest one being the top but one, and the bottom one being placed on the waist seam. As a belt is worn with this, it will be necessary to cut it rather smaller in the waist than ordinarily; otherwise surplus cloth would form in folds under the pressure of the belt; a hook is put at the hip to keep the belt in position. Flaps are placed on the hips with three buttons and notched holes, and are lined with white, as are the skirts; the pockets are placed in the pleat. We may state that notched holes have now become a thing of the past, a narrow Russia braid doing duty for this equally as well as the notched hole, it is very much easier put on and is consequently cheaper. A button is placed in the pleats as shown. The length of the strap of the skirt is made one-fifth the entire waist, being fixed at that proportion by the admiralty. This coat is used for both full and undress, and, as previously stated, the only difference for a cadet is the omission of the white end to the collar, and a notched hole and button put in its stead. We give a Table of the necessary articles for a cadet on entering H.M.S. Britannia, that being the ship where cadets are sent to undergo a course of training to enable them to pass the necessary examination to enter Her Majesty's Navy.

A midshipman's sea chest complete, with name in full on top, engraved on plain brass plate — length 3ft. 6in., breadth 2ft., height 2ft. 8in.

(It is requested that the chest may be at Dartmouth previous to the cadet's joining.)

3 Pillow Cases.
1 Hair Mattress, 5ft. 6 in. by 1ft. 9in.
3 Blankets. 6ft. 6
1 Counterpane! by
3 pair Sheets.) 4ft. 6
4 Uniform Jackets.
1 do. Trousers.
1 do. Waistcoat.
1 do. Cap, peak ½ turn down.
2 Working Uniform Suits (one of thick flannel,one of pilot cloth).
1 Uniform Working Cap, peak ½ turn down.
4 White Flannel Trousers, well shrunk.
6 pair Drawers Merino
3 White Flannel Shirts (with collar to turn down.)
3 Lambswool Under-vests.

12 White Shirts.
12 Collars.
12 pairs Merino Socks.
2 White Waist-coats.
12 Towels.
6 Night Shirts.
7 Merino Vests.
2 Black Silk Neck-ties (made up).
2 pair Braces.
pair Strong laced Boots, with thick soles.
1 Clothes Brush.
1 Sponge.
1 Carpet Bag.
1 Clothes Bag.
12 Pocket Handker-chiefs.
1 pair elastic-side Oxford Shoes, with strong soles.
1 Brush and comb.
1 Tooth Brush.
1 Nail Brush.
1 Rug (travelling).

Pea Jackets are not to be supplied, as the thick Working Jacket can be worn over the Uniform Jacket if necessary.

Clothing to be distinctly marked with the cadet's name in full.

Trousers to be made without pockets, and only one pocket on the left breast of the Jackets of the two Uniform Working Suits.

THE MORNING COAT.
Diagram 28. Figure 16.

We now come to a style of garment suitable for the youth budding into manhood, and as it is a garment of special importance from the number worn, not only by youths but by men of all sizes; and as the principles here laid down are equally applicable to the old as to the young, we will go through the system once more, and may be

we shall make points clear which are perhaps a little indefinite in the previous one. It also varies somewhat in minor details of working, so that the space devoted to it will not be lost. Commence at the back and draw line O 19, and mark off the following points O to 3½ to taste, it merely being a guide to fix the location of the shoulder seam, and which will have no effect on the fit, as any variation in this to meet the whims of a customer or the freaks of fashion, will be met, when applying the over shoulder measure. O to 9 is the depth of scye as taken on figure, O to 17 is the natural waist length, O to 19 the fashion waist, and on to 34 the full length ; if the customer is fairly hollow at the waist, come in at 17, ¾ to 1 inch, and draw the back seam in to it; draw line at right angles to point O, 3½, 9, 17; from O to 3 is ⅙ neck, come up from this point ¾, and shape back neck. If the neck has not been taken, the half waist wil do as well. From 3½ to 7¼ is the across back measure, as taken, plus seams, which usually equals one-fifth of the breast, (a too wide back is specially to be avoided). Now measure forward from point 9, the half breast measure, and whatever allowance is deemed advisable for ease, &c.; 2¼ inches is added in the present case, that being a medium quantity. Measure back from 20¼ to 12¼ the across chest measure as taken on the customer; now deduct the width of back neck from the front shoulder length, and placing the tape at point 12¼, sweep by it to find the neck point; now add 1 inch to the front shoulder length, and sweep again by this increased length from point 20¼, and wherever these arcs intersect each other is the location of the neck point; next measure up from point 9 on the back towards the shoulder seam, and see what that is, and deduct it from the over shoulder measure. Place the remainder on point 12¼, put the finger on a point 2 inches up

as at *, and make it a pivot, then sweep to find the shoulder end as at 17. We have now the scye at all points so that it can be easily reproduced, the only points requiring special attention being to make it well hollow at *, and keep it well up at sidebody. The shoulder seam of forepart may now be drawn, care being used te make it well round; the style shown on these diagrams is very good, and will produce a nice, clean fitting shoulder. Make the width of back scye about one-ninth breast, and draw the sideseam by drawing a line from this point to 17, and hollowing it ¾ of an inch on line 9; make the width of back at 17, also one-ninth breast, and shape this seam by point so obtained forming it into a graceful curve. Special attention should be paid to this seam as being so prominently seen in the garment, any defect in it would greatly detract from the grace and harmony of the garment. We have found it is always the better plan to avoid extremes of style, and recommend this method to our readers as one; that will so avoid them. Now square across from 19 to find the run of the top of the hip pleats. The sidebody may now be drawn by taking out about 1½ inches on line 17, increasing this quantity if the blades are very prominent, and *vice versa* if they are particularly flat. The sidebody should be nipped in slightly, say a bare ¼ of an inch at top, which point may be used to sweep from the back on line 19, to get the length of the bottom of sidebody, which, as will be seen, should be about ¾ of an inch lower than the back; the reason for this is not always apparent at first sight, but is explained. It will of course be understood that seams are taken off both back and sidebody, and as the back is hollow, the taking a ¼ inch off all up the sideseam will increase the length, as it must be apparent to anyone that as soon as you increase the diameter of a circle, the cir-

cumference must be increased as a matter of course. With the sidebody, however, the same principle is applied, but in the reverse way, for that being a round, a seam taken from it shortens it; hence as the one is lengthened and the other shortened in the process of seaming; so it is of importance that the sidebody should be cut long enough to allow of this. Draw a line across from this point parallel to the waist line, which forms a capital guide to get the length of waist seam in front. The waist seam may be drawn by hollowing it over the hips about 1 inch. The underarm seam may be placed in the position considered the most effective, (we prefer a narrow sidebody ourselves), and take out 1 inch at this part for a figure 4 inches smaller at waist than chest, and adding on or taking off ⅓ of the disproportion at this part as the waist increases or diminishes in its relation to the chest. Now measure across to the front the waist measure, plus 2 inches, add on a button stand, and shape the front to agree with fashion or fancy.

The Skirt

Should be drawn by squaring down from the lower line 9 inches and out 1. These quantities are suitable for all sizes, as it produces the run of the back skirts at a given angle, which is suitable for an ordinary well developed figure, but should be increased for a person with very prominent seat, and vice versa. Draw a line from the bottom of the sidebody, through point 1 out from 9, and round the back of skirt about ½ an inch which should be well worked forward over to the hips in making; a bare ¼ inch may be hollowed out between skirt and forepart at point 1, and a trifle may be taken out of waist seam at front. The skirt should have at least an inch of fulness beyond the combined width of sidebody and forepart; the run of the front should be made to agree with the forepart. The breast pocket is put on a level with the bottom of scye slanting slightly downwards, and at least 1 inch in front of the most forward part of scye. The sleeve as explained on Diagram 9, will suit this so it will be only necessary we should turn our attention to

THE DRESS COAT.
Diagram 29. Figure 17.

In order to complete the garment. Point A is the height at which the coat is desired to button, and we require a collar with a 1¼ stand and 1¾ fall. B is a ¼ of an inch less than the height of stand above the hollowest part of the gorge, and line A B C is drawn. D is the difference between the height of stand and the depth of fall below C, and line D B A forms the crease line. D to E is the stand which is then drawn from D to the hollowest part of gorge, and following it round to G where a seam is added. The shape of the collar end at H must be left to the taste of the operator, to form it in accordance with the turn, so as to produce the effect desired. F is the depth of the fall above D, and is drawn from F to H. This is a collar system which adapts itself to almost all styles and widths of collar, from the Dress Coat to the Overcoat with the wide collar. It requires very little working up, and has the advantage of adding additional spring at the fall edge; when the fall becomes deeper, a result which must commend itself to all thoughtful minds. Of course there are styles of collar which cannot be produced by this system, and which will be treated in connection with such garments they are usually worn on. We now come to

It will not be necessary to go over the various points, as they are produced in the same way as for a Morning Coat, with the exception that they are usually made rather close-fitting and are sometimes a trifle narrower in the back. From 9 to 19½ is only 1½ inches over the breast measure, but this is ½ an inch from the actual centre of the front of the garment, and from which the sweep to obtain the position of the neck point is cast. The gorge is lowered quite an inch, and the waist is made to the net size, as they are never worn buttoned: The lapel is cut by drawing a straight line and hollowing it 1 inch back at the bottom as shown. The top is made about 2 to 2¼ inches wide and pointed upwards, and the middle or belly part is made about 2½ to 3¼ wide; the bottom is made 1½. It is generally advisable to cut these lapels on the double at the outer edge, which is arranged by taking out a large V at the top, and keeping it rather to one side, so that it shall be out of sight; this will greatly facilitate getting a much cleaner thin edge, a feature well worthy of notice at such a part of a Dress Coat.

The skirt is cut in the same way as the Morning Coat, the length of the strap being generally fixed at ⅓ of the width across at the waist, and the bottom edge fixed at about 1 inch less than a half, and the front edge slightly rounded. The width of the strap is generally made 1½ inches, and as will be noticed, it only comes to the lapel seam.

BLAZER, or CRICKET and BOATING JACKET.
Diagram 31. Figure 18.

There are few young gentlemen to be found at the present time who do not patronize their school or club blazer, let it be either, for cricket, lawn tennis, or boating, and few garments could be more appropriate for outdoor exercise. Being thin and comparatively loose fitting, they are not oppressive in wear; and as they are made from woollen material, they do not expose the wearer to any danger of catching cold, such as would be experienced from the use of cotton. They are made from almost every conceivable colour and combination of colours, and finished in a variety of ways; it being the general custom, when a club is started, to go to their tailor, and get him to have their colours printed specially, and reserved for their exclusive use; and in a few cases they are registered. Swaisland's are generally supposed to be the best printers of this class of flannel, and their goods may be obtained from most of the best wholesale houses. There is, however, a new make of woven flannel in the market, but not having tested the same we are unable to express any opinion on it. When made from striped flannels, they are generally finished in the way indicated on the diagram with three patch pockets, sleeves lined, and facings and seams felled down; although many houses make them almost entirely by machine, in order to reduce the price as much as possible; the buttons are usually covered with same material. Many clubs, however, adopt a self-colour, and bind it with contrasting colours of ribbon joined together, in which case they generally have the monogram or crest of their club worked on the breast pocket, a method which is very popular with the Oxford and Cambridge College Clubs. There is just one point that requires special mention in dealing with striped flannels with more than two stripes. It is necessary to treat these the same way as if they had a way of the wool to them, *i.e.*, split and turn one part, otherwise one side of the coat will have the pattern running differently to the

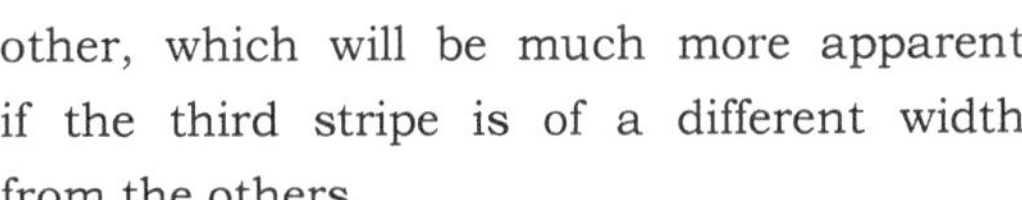

other, which will be much more apparent if the third stripe is of a different width from the others.

Turning to the diagram, it will be noticed the back is cut whole, and with that exception, cut exactly the same as the Lounge described previously; they are not intended to fit very closely or define the waist to a nicety, as the extra size produced by the back being left whole, just gives it a character. If, however, it is wished to follow the figure rather more than it would as in this diagram, it will be necessary to take out rather more at 6½, 8, but this must not be done to excess, it being very much better to take out a fish under the arms to bring it to the size of waist desired, this being a very much safer plan than to reduce it too much at the sideseam. The sleeve used would be the same as shown for the Lounge.

THE CAP,
Diagrams 32 and 33,

Is frequently made from the same material as the Jacket, hence our giving a diagram to enable the tailor to supply every want of his customer in this direction The stripes are generally made to run round. although that by no means necessarily follows. The shape generally preferred is that known as the Eton; it being very largely used at this training ground of our aristocracy. The special feature in them is that they come over the back of the head rather more than ordinarily; the system for producing them is as follows: O to 11½ half the circumference of the head, plus seams; this is then divided into three parts, viz., the front side and back; the front is ¼ inch above line at O, and the back is lowered ¾; O to 5⅝ is half the distance O 11½; point 5⅝ is half 11½ from 5½; and 2 and 9¼ are placed rather over ⅙ from either end, so as to make the seam nearest to the centre piece the shortest.

The Peak,
Diagram 33,

May be reproduced exactly as shown, and making O 6 rather over half 11½. Of course it will be readily understood this only represents the half of the peak, the part at 1½ 3½ being cut on the crease. In making up it will be as well to put a stay tape round the bottom edge, and keep it to the size of the head. The cap itself is lined with white Silesia or Silk, and the peak lined with the same material as the cap is made from, a piece of very stiff buckram or leather being put through the peak to keep it firm.

THE COVERT COAT.
Diagram 34. Figure 19.

We now come to deal with Overcoats and certainly there is no more effective style than the Covert Coat, for such purposes as riding, walking, &c. It has a natty, smart appearance, totally distinct from the longer styles. It is also, made rather closer-fitting than the ordinary overcoat, but this will be gathered from the diagrams. One of the special feature in this garment is the style in which the seams are finished; they are seldom left plain, but more frequently strapped with a piece of the same material cut on the reverse way of the wool about 1 inch wide, which is then serged together, laid on top of the seams, and stitched close on the edge. The reason it is cut the wrong way of the wool is to make it show up more prominently than it would if the pile runs the same way. When we speak of the reverse way of the wool, we do not mean upside down, but with the pile running round the figure; of course there are other ways besides this, such as slating generally used with Meltons, and such materials as will stand raw edge. Then again, there are raised seams which merely consist

of turning the seam aside and stitching it from the outside instead of pressing it open; whilst others are stitched on either side of the seam after it is pressed open. In our opinion the first style is the most effective, especially with drab Venetians, such as Covert Coats are usually made from. The hindarm of the sleeve is frequently made to run with the shoulder seam so that the strapping shall go in one continuous line; and when that is desired, it will be necessary to take some from the topside sleeve and add to the under, and by that means adjust the run of the sleeve at whatever position you may desire. It is frequently a difficulty to put the strapping down the forearm seam, and it may not be out of place if we give a plan whereby it is fairly easy. This consists of preparing the strapping and stitching it to the topside previous to the seam being sewn, and then stitch down the other side of the strapping also before joining the seam, after which the seam may be either lapped under the strapping or seamed in the ordinary way, after which it will be necessary to fell the undersleeve to the strapping, with as private a stitch as possible. The bottom of the cuff is invariably finished with 5 or 6 rows of sewing, which should have a piece of domett or padding underneath to throw up the sewing, which should also be done before closing the seam at forearm. The rows of stitching are usually placed the same distance apart as those on the strapping, the edges, pockets, and pocket mouths being finished with two rows of sewing in the same way. They are generally made up fly front, which is sometimes, but by no means always, stitched in with two rows of sewing, which should on no account go through the facing, as it detracts very much from the neatness of finish; slits are left at the side, and a facing should be left on the forepart for this. Four out pockets,

all finished with flaps, and a tab for the collar, see diagram 35, are all features of this coat. Turning to the cutting, it will be seen it is cut to a size larger than the Lounge, adding ⅜ to front and over shoulder measures, but of the same style, and 1¾ left all down the front for a button stand; extra spring is left over the hips, and, as will be seen, the front is carried down straight. If the measures have been taken on the customer as in the ordinary way, it will be necessary to make the following additions: add 1 inch a side to the chest measure, so that from 9¼ to 21¼ will be 1 inch more than for the Lounge, that being the quantity it is always safe to allow for an Overcoat when the measure has been taken on the vest, which plan we always advise, as it will be patent to all that various coats will measure differently; and as we wish to produce a garment that will suit the customer over the average style of coat, it will always be safe to get as near his actual measure as possible, and then make such allowance as experience teaches is correct. This quantity we believe to be 1 inch a side, which is divided as follows: one-fifth at back, two-fifths across chest, and two-fifths under the arms, but if that is not so easy as quarter inches, then we would give ¼ inch extra across the back, ⅜ under the arm, and ⅜ across the chest. This should be increased to 1¼ side extra at the waist, as owing to the pockets, &c., the waist increases faster than the chest; use the other cross-measures in exactly the same way as for a Lounge, adding ⅜ to ½ an inch to both front and over shoulders, and then deepen the scye ½ an inch; if ⅝ it will be better in a stout material. The sleeves should also be made quite ½ or ¾ of an inch wider at elbow and cuff than for a Lounge, on both top and underside. It is always wise to err on the side of a too-long fall edge to the collar than the reverse, for, being exposed to all inclemen-

cies of the weather, they would soon shrink if any amount of stretching were necessary to bring them to a correct shape. These hints are applicable to all Overcoats, and as we shall have occasion to refer to them again, we wish to impress them on our readers' minds. Covert Coats are usually made from 2 to 4 inches longer than the Lounge, one of the great features being their shortness, as if made long they at once lose their distinctive character, and become a short Chesterfield.

Overcoat, Ulster, &c.
Diagram 37. Figures 20, 21, 22, and 23.

These are produced in the same way as just described, either by taking the sectional measures for a size larger, and adding ⅜ to the front and over-shoulder measure, or if you have the opportunity of measuring the customer yourself to make the necessary addition as described for a Covert Coat. Chesterfields and Ulsters are made looser-fitting rather than the Covert Coat, as a rule, so that if a very close fit is desired, it will be as well to take that as the model, and merely add to the length. It may be as well to recapitulate the variations to be made from the measures for an Overcoat:

Allow 3½ over chest.
Allow 3½ over waist.
Add ¼ inch to cross back measure.
Add ⅜ inch to cross chest measure.
Add ⅜ inch to cross front shoulder.
Add ⅜ inch to cross over shoulder.
Deepen scye ½ an inch.

Make natural waist ¼ inch lower, and make sleeve ½ inch wider at elbow and cuff and ½ inch longer. The spring over the hips in this case is arranged by coming in from the waist at side 6, and dropping 1 inch, and then drawing the lower part of sideseam at right angles to this as shown; this may either be used in units or inches, as it makes no difference, both producing the same angle. It will be noticed that in addition to the allowance of 1 inch a-side for being an Overcoat, 2½ inches is allowed for making up, which will be found about right for all Winter goods, but too much for thin Worsteds and Venetians as used for Summer Overcoats, 2 inches will be quite enough for these. The solid outline of this diagram illustrates the allowance usually left beyond the centre line for a fly front, such as figure 20, being 2 to 2¼ inches, and which will necessitate the buttons standing 3 to 3½ inches back from the edge of the right forepart, or the same distance behind the breast line as the eye of the hole is in front of it. For a button through coat, single-breasted, as on figure 20, it will only be necessary to allow 1½ inches beyond the breast line, whilst for a D.B. illustrated by the dash line in front of diagram 37, it will be necessary to allow 3 to 3½ inches, and find the position of buttons as just described. The slit at back should start 9 inches down from the natural waist, and the back tacking allowed as shown; marking out 1¼ from the back at that part, and drawing a straight line from O at top through the 1¼. This will give the correct run to the back tacking. As worn at present, it is turned in to run level with the back seam, which is certainly much neater than when they were made with a step at that part. The fish under the arm may be omitted for Ulsters, and the sideseam hardly so much suppressed, as it is not intended to fit as close as the Chester, the length being continued by adding on at bottom to the desired extent. In order to get the front of a length sufficient to agree with the back, it will be necessary to make it ¾ of an inch longer than the back, measuring from line 9½ downwards, and independent of any variation which may exist from that line upwards, and which would arise from the various

positions of different customers. Care should be taken not to put the pockets too low, as that makes it inconvenient for the wearer; at the same time it is advisable to guard against them being too high, as that does not look in accordance with good taste. Some of our best firms, Poole's, for instance, of Savile Row, leave these till the garment is tried on, when they mark the position they consider the most suitable, when the garment is on, and this is certainly a very capital plan. Others again take a measure for this purpose, in order that they may be put in before the garment is tried on, as when trying on it is out of the question to alter their position. Others put the sleeve with the forearm at the forearm pitch, and mark the pocket mouth about 3½ inches above the bottom of sleeve, whilst the majority leave it to their individual judgment and taste, fixing them in some such a position as shown. It will be noticed the ticket pocket of this is brought more forward than the hip pocket, but this is by no means a regulation style, there being as many put in with the ticket pocket level with the front of those at hip, and in some cases they are put very near the front, so that they are under the fly and so out of sight. The position of the breast pocket is found in the same manner as for a Lounge. In putting in the hip and ticket pockets, it is always as well to put a back and front facing, as that takes most of the wear.

Diagram 41.

Conveys a capital idea of how these coats are made up inside, the shaded part along the bottom being an inlay to which the lining is felled. A linen bridle is put along the crease row at B, and in some firms the ends of the shoulders are built up with two or three thicknesses of canvas nicely graded as at A, but in such a case it will be necessary to cut rather more on the shoulder end.

It will be noticed that pleats are put in the lining down the front shoulder under the arm, and down the back, and the fly kept a seam behind the front edge, the stay for the hip pockets being either carried in to the scye or to the sideseam; either plan will do, but it is scarcely necessary to use both. A V of silk is put in the front of scye to allow ample room at that part, the in breast pockets should be jetted top and bottom, and faced. The two hip pockets of an Overcoat should always be either cloth or chamois leather, as Silesia feels poor and cold to put the hands in. The lining as represented, is a woollen plaid, which should always be well shrunk before being put in, or it will give a good deal of trouble.

The Sleeve,
Diagram 40,

Is produced on precisely the same lines as described previously, the only variation being the increased width of both elbow and wrist by ¾ of an inch, and the cuff stitched as shown. It should always be made a point to flash-baste the lining to both seams in all coats, but more especially is this necessary with Overcoats, for it relieves the drag which is sure to occur in putting on or taking off the coat, and especially so when silk sleeve linings are not used, either on account of expense or wear. If Italian cloth is used it should be cut with sleeve running across the material, not lengthways.

The Cape,
Diagram 38.

If we may judge by the number of applications for a really reliable Cape System, we must come to the conclusion there are very few who can cut a good-fitting Cape. We trust this one will be of service to them; it has answered our purpose and given satisfaction to hundreds; and being very simple and reliable, we have no doubt it will be a valuable addition. Draw a square as per dotted lines, or rather two lines at right angles, and place the back with the back seam on one line, and then place the forepart down with the breast line on the dotted line, so that the shoulder points are at least 1 inch apart. Mark round the neck and shoulder of back, and the gorge and shoulder of forepart, taking out a V as at ¾. The inch of fulness should be fulled on to the forepart in the same style as a sleeve. Now continue the shoulder seam right through to bottom, and make the width of back on a level with the natural waist at about ²⁄₃ of breast; a trifle more or less is of no consequence. Take out a V of 3 or 4 inches at bottom according to the degree of closeness it is desired to make the Cape to fit. Make the length of back to customer's wishes, and then deduct the distance the shoulder seam is below the level of neck (as O 3½ diagram 37) from this, and get the length of side by applying this measure from the end of shoulder seam at X. Make the front length ¾ of an inch longer from O than back, and draw the bottom edge by these points. Add on a button stand if it is desired it should button over up the fronts, or if it is wished to wear it with a collar and turn as in figure 18, cut it to the dot and dash line, which should be about 1½ or 2 inches behind the breast line. Some may ask the reason of the V at 1¾; it is necessary to provide sufficient room for the shoulder and avoid surplus width at the bottom, and this is the only method of producing this unless the back is made much wider, and the seam made to run exactly over the shoulder, which does not give nearly such a stylish appearance as this method. In cutting from the cloth the back should be cut on the crease, and the pattern (check or stripe) made to run straight with the front edge of forepart, so that it is only cut through at the shoulder seams. This may be continued to any length desired by merely adjusting the length as described above. If a fuller Cape is desired, swing the forepart more forward by reducing the distance between A O, still keeping the shoulders in the same position; this may be done till the shoulders are brought together, and there is no seam at A X, which then produces a very full Cape known as the Three-quarter Circular Cape.

Hoods.
Diagram 39.

Hoods are produced in a very similar way to capes, and we here illustrate two different styles, the dot and dash line being the jelly-bag hood, and the longer and solid outline being the cape hood. The back and forepart are placed together, with the ends of the shoulders touching as per dotted lines, and the run of the neck is thus obtained; this is really the only part of the hood that fits, all the other being purely a question of taste and style. The cape hood is very suitable for gentlemen; F G H being sewn together up to G, and I H is sewn to the corresponding part on the other side, the V at neck C B D is sewn up, and that part up from I to E is drawn in with elastic or cord. If wanted to put on or off, it will be best to sew the neck to a narrow band and fasten it to the stand of the collar with holes and buttons, the seam coming just on the top of the collar seam. They are sometimes lined but not often, that plan being more frequently adopted for ladies. The jelly-bag is a much smaller style of hood, and is pointed at the bottom, it makes up in the same way, and is very close-fitting to the head in wear. These are the two principal styles of hoods worn by gentlemen. Other types being more of a fancy nature, are more suitable for ladies.

The easiest way of producing this very comfortable style of garment is by a Chesterfield block, which is shown on diagram 35, by the dotted lines. The old style of Inverness was very loose and baggy, but the present style is to have it much closer fitting, with just enough room in the cape to allow of the arms being put "akimbo".

The great feature in dealing with an Inverness, is to avoid a wide back, as that is very apt to produce a dragging in the wing. The back is cut on the crease, it being drawn by going out 1 inch from the natural waist of a Chester, and drawing from top of neck through it to the bottom; the sideseam of back is squared down the same width as at the top, quite straight.

The forepart is cut exactly the same as the forepart of the Chester in front, but with additional width at sideseam, it being made to overlap the back at waist, according to the degree of fulness desired in the back. If wanted to fit moderately easy it should overlap about 1½ or 2 inches, and be continued through to the bottom by drawing a straight line from the shoulder point of back; if, however, it is required to fit into the waist and define the figure at that part, it will then be necessary to shape the sideseam, as for a Chesterfield, and taking out about 1 inch at natural waist, then springing over the seat as described for that garment; but it should always be borne in mind that the closer the body of the coat fits, the more spring will be required in the wing, in order to produce the necessary ease for the arms. If it is desired to put sleeves to this garment, it will be best to cut all the scye in one with the forepart, making the shoulder the full width, and carrying it round to the two dots at back, so that the sideseam may still run up to the shoulder, and allow of the cape being sewn in with it. When worn without sleeves, the armhole may be enlarged to any extent, but if it is desired to be fairly close-fitting, it is advisable to keep it about 1 or 2 inches above the natural waist; a 1½ inch button stand is generally added, it being customary to make this garment to button through.

Patch pockets are generally looked upon as the correct thing, and are made large and roomy, usually being placed in the position shown.

We will now describe the special feature of this garment.

The Wing.
Diagram 44.

A very great latitude is allowed in the amount of spring given to this, but it should be borne in mind that the closer the body of this garment is cut, the fuller it is necessary to cut the wing in order to avoid that contraction so frequently experienced in these when the arms are raised. The diagrams show a wing arranged to agree with the body as illustrated on diagram 43; it is cut by placing the back and forepart down as shown by dotted lines, and then taking the sleeve and placing it with the forearm at the forearm pitch, allowing it to overlap about 1 inch, so that it touches the scye up to midway between the top of front shoulder and the forearm pitch. Now mark round the top of sleeve, and make a mark as at * * where the hindarm comes, so that it may be put in to the back pitch of sleeve. Now put the finger on this spot, and swing the sleeve round till the amount of spring desired is obtained; in this instance it is brought to the level of scye line on back, or say 2½ to 3½ inches over the half breast, from centre line of front, and the wing is drawn to that point by the hindarm of sleeve; the lower part requires a little additional spring as

shown; one of the best guides being to turn the sleeve over, so that the forearm rests on that part of the wing already found, and then draw the lower portion by it. The corner is rounded off and left loose from the sideseam for a few inches as illustrated, to where the stitching of edge terminates. The length of the wing is also arranged by the sleeve, it being usual to let them come to just cover the coat sleeve , so the back part of wing is found by the sleeve when swung round, as per the most backward dotted lines, and the side with the sleeve laid in the position in which it was first laid, and whence it is continued across almost straight; 1½ inches of spring is added on the front beyond the forepart as shown, to prevent any tendency to open at that part. The fulness at top of wing should be put in exactly the same as with a sleeve head, and if necessary the V may be cut a little deeper. In making, a stay should be put at the part where the wing is finished at sideseam, and also at the terminating point at neck, it being frequently left loose 2 or 3 inches from the centre line, so that it may be easier thrown back over the shoulder. The wing is generally lined with silk, which is sometimes brought to the edge, and in others the front is faced. The Cape may be either made to button through or fasten with a fly. The general rule with Inverness Capes is to make them to button to the throat with a Prussian collar.

Diagram 45,

Which is produced as follows: all garments that are finished with this style of collar fastening up to the throat, it is not necessary to take the gorge into consideration beyond its length, hence the diagram may be taken as a standard pattern for this collar. Draw line O 8, which is perfectly straight, and make it the length of the gorge;

come up from 8 1 inch, and draw the sewing to edge of the collar, as from 1 to O; O should be just above 1¼ at the other end of line 8. Now mark the stand upwards from this, say 1¼ at back, and from ½ to ¾ in front, and draw the crease edge; the fall may then be added to taste, in this case being made 1¾ inches at back, and 1½ in front; hollow the centre of back about ¼ inch, and spring it forward at 1½ as shown. Many Invernesses, however, are worn with a small turn, and to some this is a bit of a puzzle. There are two (if not more) ways of doing this: the one is to cut the forepart of diagram 43 off in the shape of a no-collar vest, and in making up make the turn on the wing, fastening the forepart to it to within about 1 inch of the centre or breast line, that being sufficient to steady the wing and at the same time allows plenty of ease for buttoning both. The other method is to cut the Cape away to about 1 inch behind the breast, the disadvantage to this way being that it does not allow of the Cape being buttoned across the front, which is overcome to a certain extent by putting tabs at the bottom corner to fasten it to buttons put on the forepart. There is another style of Inverness worn at present, with the Cape coming all round the back, but we shall refer to this later on under the title of the Scarborough, so that we will proceed with the next garment, viz.,

THE DRESSING GOWN.
Diagrams 46 and 47. Figure 26.

The diagram for this is very nearly self-explanatory, as it shows the style in which these are not only cut but made. Of course a great variety of styles exists in the manner in which they are trimmed, but there are few more effective or popular than our illustrations. As will be seen, the cuffs and collars are finished with quilted satin, usually of a contrasting colour, and the edges corded to match the satin, which terminates at the bottom with a crow's toe, this method is also used for the trimming of the cuff above the satin; as will be noticed, the collar is of the roll form, a style which is invariably adopted for Dressing Gowns, although occasionally we see them fastening to the throat with a stand collar, but this is the exception rather than the rule. The fronts and pockets are also trimmed with cord, the latter being corded round and terminated with a crow's toe, the same style of ornament is also adopted for the cords across the breast, together with an eye on either side in the centre; the cord is left in loops beyond on the left side, so that it may go over the barrels or olivets placed on, or a little distance from, the crow's toe. A woollen girdle is put through loops placed one on either side, which are sometimes supplemented by one at the back; this is also of the same colour as the satin and cord. Turning our attention to the cutting, they are cut to the easy side at breast, and decidedly loose-fitting at the waist. They are cut with 2½ inches allowance for making up at chest, and are made 1 inch wider at back than dotted line, and the forepart is made to overlap the back also 1 inch at the natural waist, which lines are carried straight through to the bottom; the amount of overlap in this case is 3 inches, which may be reduced if desired. It will be noticed all the other points are produced in the same way as the Lounge, and the scye deepened a trifle, say ¼ of an inch. The sleeve should be made to the easy side, at least ½ an inch wider at both elbow and wrist than for a Lounge. The roll collar is cut by the same system as explained in diagram 30, with the exception that no step is taken out, the collar being made to form one continuous run with the front. These garments are required more for ease than closeness of fit, so that the

only part at which it will be necessary to pay special attention will be the shoulders and neck; the back, as will be seen, is cut on the crease. The fronts are generally faced a little way back, and the pockets are patched on the inside.

THE CHORISTER'S CASSOCK.
Diagrams 48 and 49. Figure 27.

This is a garment the tailor is frequently called upon to make, it being used rather extensively, and is the same as worn by the verger, pew opener, and sometimes the clergy themselves wear the same style. It is cut as a very long Chester, with full skirts, and sufficient left on for box plaits at the centre of back and sideseams. It should be made rather easy fitting, in fact, may be treated exactly as a Chester, with the exception that it is only worn over the vest. The waist is only intended to slightly define the figure, so that it is not made at all close to the measures, and, as will be seen, only 1 inch of suppression taken out between the back and forepart at sideseam. The spring of sideseam at bottom is got by coming in from it on either side at natural waist line 6 inches, and dropping down 1 or 1¼ and then drawing this seam at right angles; this will readily be gathered from the diagram. A pocket is sometimes put in the pleats at side, and a small ticket or cash pocket is invariably put in the forepart. The one great feature about the garment is to keep it close up at the neck, as any excess of size at that part would detract from the fit. The collar is of the ordinary stand form, and the cuff either left plain or made to form a gauntlet-style of cuff as shown on diagram 49. A button stand of 1¼ inches is allowed on, so that the buttons may come just down the centre. These run somewhere about 40 for a man of 5ft. 8in.; some contend they should be just 39 to agree with the 39 articles, but this is not looked upon as regulations; they are, however, placed very close together, very little over 1¼ inches apart, and are generally arranged for every one to button down to a little below waist, say the first 15, and below that every other one. They are usually lined low enough to cover the top of the pleats, which thus brings it to about the hip. A facing is put down the front from the neck point to about 3 or 4 inches wide at bottom; this takes the holes and buttons. The buttons are usually a 28 line flexible, sometimes oval top, this size being about midway between a coat and vest size. The materials generally used for these are fine Serge, Russel Cord, Worsted Diagonal, or fine Alpaca. A small space shows between the collar ends, when finished, say of about 1 or 1½ inches, although a variation of opinion exists as to this. To get the correct length for these, we know some of the London specialists in this branch make it a rule to take the total height of the customer, and deduct 10 inches; they also ask the customer the size linen collar he wears, and adjusts the Cassock collar to agree with it. We now come to another semi-clerical garment, viz.,

THE CHORISTER'S SURPLICE.
Diagram 50. Figure 28.

This is a garment tailors are not often called upon to make, for two reasons: one is, they are more generally supplied ready made by firms who devote themselves to this particular branch, and secondly, to the fact that those who have them make them last a very long time, as being made of linen they wear out very slowly. However, we felt it would be adding very greatly to the value of the present work, if we gave diagrams and instructions how these are made, as it being only an occasional garment, few tailors would have the necessary knowledge at their finger ends, and so

would be glad of any information obtainable on this topic. The cutting of a surplice is a very easy matter, it being the usual custom to use one pattern for all medium sizes, and merely adjusting its length at the bottom, so that it will be better to reproduce this one by the aid of graduated tapes, to agree with the chest measure. We think the diagram is fully explanatory, and we have placed the various parts exactly as they go together. It does not come close round the neck, but shows the cassock above some 3 or 4 inches. The sleeve as will be seen is cut upon the crease from 8 to 29, and goes up into and forms part of the neck, as with the old Raglan sleeve. The top part is cut much shorter than the back as illustrated at 2. The back and front are both cut on the crease, but as the linen is only 36 inches wide on the single, it will be found necessary to put wheel pieces on the back, the front just coming out of the width.

The sleeve will be able to be got out of the material if it is opened out, but if any piecing is necessary, it must be done at the bottom of the sleeve. In making up, the sideseams are first sewn, and then the sleeves put in from the neck end in the same manner in which they are placed on the diagram. When about 4 inches from the sideseam, a gusset 4 inches square, as diagram 51, is inserted, and the remainder of sleeve sewn together, and so forming an underarm seam to the sleeve. The bottom sleeves are finished with a ½ or ⅝ inch hem, and the bottom is finished in like manner, but rather wider, the neck being done ditto; but in this case it is necessary to sew on a piece, and so form a false hem in the same way we case trouser bottoms. In order to get sufficient spring on the outside edge, it will be necessary to cut this piece on the bias, or, of course, it may be cut exactly the same as neck of surplice, but in any case it must be made so that it lies quite smooth and fair all round. The seams of this are sewn in the same way as a shirt is usually done, viz., seamed and turned over, and felled or stitched. The neck being cut so large, enables the garment being put on or off with ease, so that holes and buttons are not necessary, as in the case of those styles for clergymen, that fasten right up to the neck. There are many styles of surplice, but this is the one generally known as the chorister's.

For the sake of economy, the back is arranged with the selvage edges sewn together and coming down the back, and so saving material as mentioned.

The material generally used for these is linen.

LIVERY GARMENTS.

We now come to deal with another speciality, viz., those garments worn by the page boy, and the tiger or groom, and illustrated on

Dias. 52, 53, 54 & 55. Figs. 29 & 30.

Taking first the Page's Jacket, we find it is cut very much in the shape of an Eton Jacket, but made to fasten up the front, and the neck finished with a stand collar, the principal variation being a rather wider back than for the Eton. As this is made to fit quite close, care must be taken to form ample spring over the hips, it being decidedly preferable to err on the side of too much rather than too little spring. As these jackets are seldom worn with a vest, care must be taken not to cut them too large, for although they are usually interlined with wadding and quilted all over the forepart, and occasionally the back, too, yet this hardly makes up for the want of the vest, so that we have found 1¾ a-side over the breast measure to be quite sufficient. It will of course be noticed that the back is

cut on the crease, and like the Eton, cut with a point at bottom, which usually runs about 3½ inches below the waist. Like all garments that button up the front, this should be cut with only about ⅝ or ¾ of an inch beyond the breast line on the button-hole side, and an extra button stand allowed on; by this arrangement the buttons come exactly up the centre of the figure when buttoned, as the eye of the hole comes just on the breast line. Care should be taken to get the gorge the right size of neck, as it is a very unsightly fault, and a tedious alteration when it is too large. The collar is generally fastened at the neck with hooks and eyes, and sometimes a button and notched hole is put in the end, as illustrated on the midshipman's diagram 23. The buttons down the front are arranged so that there are about 16, but sometimes there are three rows of studs, in which case they are plugged through the foreparts, both up the front and over the shoulder, the garment being actually fastened with hooks and eyes, and the buttons or studs down the front for ornament only. One of the points connected with these buttons is to put them just thick enough to preserve one unbroken line, but there is a danger of putting them too thick, which must be specially guarded against, as in such case they present a very crooked appearance. When these jackets are edged they are usually edged up the front, round the collar and cuffs, and sometimes, but by no means always, round the bottom. The style of cuff varies somewhat, but that shown on diagram 54 is the one more generally adopted, and which may be justly looked upon as the livery cuff as it is universally used for all kinds of Livery Coats. As will be seen it is either a cuff formed, or a row of stitching 2 inches from the bottom, and a hole and button put above and one below, so that when the edges are piped, there is

a piping also along the top of this cuff. The other style which is occasionally adopted, is the pointed cuff, the front being brought up rather nearer the forearm than the back, and along the top of which the piping runs. When this style is adopted, it is customary to dispense with holes and buttons at the cuff.

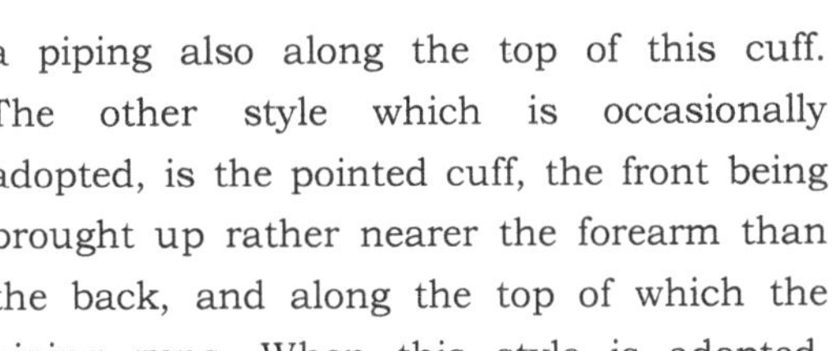

Stand Collar,
Diagram 55.

Garments that have a stand collar invariably button up to the throat, so that it is not necessary to take the gorge into consideration here, hence one pattern of stand collar does for all sizes by merely varying the width at top and the length at back. The system for producing them is as follows: Draw line O 8 the length collar is desired, and measure up from 8, 1 inch, and draw sewing-to-edge by points thus obtained, letting it join line O 8 about half-way across from O to 1½ is the depth of collar required at the back, and 1, 2¼ is the depth of collar required in the front; come in from 2½ ½ an inch, and draw the top edge as shown. As a rule it is immaterial whether these collars have a seam up the back as at O 1½ but when, as in the present instance, the back has no seam in it, the collar should be arranged to follow suit, as it is by no means a necessity. We find buckram is very much better than canvas to put through these, as it is highly essential they should retain their stiffness, otherwise they have a very sloppy appearance. An inlay is left all along the bottom of a Page's Jacket, and the breast pocket, which is usually placed in the left breast, should have the mouth to run vertically, that is, up and down, this enables the hand to use it with greater ease; when the edges are not piped they are left bluff, that being the universal custom with Liveries. The Page's trousers are of the ordinary close-fitting type, and may be made rather smarter fitting than is the rule for other Liveries, and as the seat is fully exposed to view, care must be taken to avoid having any surplus material, either in width or length, although of course sufficient width must be left for ease or stooping, &c.; they are always made fly front, and when the edges of jacket are piped, the sideseam of trousers are done to match.

The Groom's Frock,

This, as will be seen, is a close-fitting single-breasted Frock, to button 6 up the front; this number is sometimes reduced to 5, but the first is generally looked upon as the regulation number. It is produced exactly as previously described for the Morning Coat, with the exception that it is made to fasten right down the front, and the waist is made to fit tight, as any excess of width at that part would readily show itself when worn with a belt as they generally are. The variation in the skirt is done to produce more fulness, and as will be readily gathered from an examination of the diagram, no difference exists behind the sidebody from the system, as laid down for the Morning Coat skirt, it being readily followed that both styles should fit exactly the same at the pleats. The variation then takes place at the front, where it is allowed to overlap the forepart 2 inches at least; if a very full skirt is required this quantity may be increased to 3 inches, but as a general rule 2 inches will be sufficient for this class of skirt, the run of the front may then be obtained by placing the square with one arm resting on the hip button at bottom corner of sidebody, and the other end raised as much above the level of the skirt seam in front as that part overlaps the forepart; this will give the correct angle at which the front should be drawn. Another way is to put the forepart in a closing

position with the skirt, and draw the front by that; either method will produce satisfactory results, so that our readers may adopt which plan they consider best. A short pointed side edge is put at the pleats 9 inches long in the form shown on diagram, with the centre button a trifle nearer the top than the bottom one. This at one time was used as an entrance to the pocket, but the present custom is to put the pockets in the pleats. The edges are either left bluff or piped with a contrasting colour. When the latter course is adopted, the fronts, collars, cuffs, back skirt, and side edges are piped, the bottom edge being left plain; seamed and pressed open, always makes a neater bluff edge than a felled one, both of which methods are in vogue by first class Livery houses. The style of cuff used is the same as shown on diagram 54. It may be as well to mention in connection with these that it is the custom to put all linings of a very plain character, and for this reason wadding or padding of any description is only flash-basted in; this applies to all Livery garments except Page's. Groom's Vests are generally made of the roll collar style, often with sleeves, the material used being either the same as the coat, or a striped Valencia; and when the latter is adopted the stripes run up and down the figure.

The Breeches are generally made from white Buckskin cloth, and in style of cut resemble the Gents' Riding Breeches shown on diagram 74, but are not so extreme if the line by which to draw the front is dropped from 12 at side from ¾ to 1 inch, instead of 1½ that will be quite sufficient. Like the Gent's, the Groom's Breeches button to the front of knee, and the top button should be just about the small the tack being placed 1 inch below the knee, and the top button 1 inch below that, three buttons show above the top boots and two above the leggings. An inch should be allowed for fulness on the topsides at knee, and a similar amount allowed on the undersides above the level of crotch to allow of it being fulled on to form a receptacle for the seat. They are generally made close-fitting as regards the size of thigh and leg, and the fronts made in whole fall style, but this must by no means be taken for granted, as fly fronts are made for this class of servant.

Although top boots are generally worn, yet gaiters are often adopted, diagrams of which will be found in the Federation Prize Essay on Trouser Cutting.

The instructions laid down up to this point, although applied more particularly to Youth's Jackets, Coats, &c., embody principles which may be applied with equal success to all sizes both large and small, the working of the system making all the necessary changes of its own accord, with the exception of corpulency; hints on the treatment of which and other abnormalities will be found in the "Cutter's Practical Guide", Part II., at the end of the volume.

Vests

We now come to deal with another branch of cutting, and for which a further adaptation of the system is necessary. A vest is really nothing more nor less than an undercoat, and the same principles which apply to the cutting of coats will apply with equal force to them. One thing, however, will be soon apparent to even the most unobservant, viz., that they are not required so large. In the system as explained below, and referred to in diagrams 56 and 57, this variation is made by reducing the width across chest ½ an inch, and making it only 1½ inches over the breast measure from the centre of the back to the breast line, whilst it is just as well to reduce the front and over shoulder measures ¼ inch, but we will treat more of this in dealing with the system. In practice it has been our almost universal custom to produce our

Vest by the Coat or Jacket Pattern, Diagram 56.

Inasmuch as they are worn over and have to fit the same portion of the body as the coat. The method we adopt is as follows: chalk round the pattern at the shoulders, back seam and breast line in front. Hollow the back ½ to 1 inch at waist, and being equal to half the suppression taken out at sideseam of coat, with the view of providing a receptacle for the blades; and measure from the back seam forward ½ vest and ¾ of an inch on the level of scye line, and ½ waist and ¾ of an inch at natural waist; then apply the same at the front, but measuring back from the breast line fill up the neck point a trifle, say ¼ of an inch; and shorten the shoulder right across a ¼ inch; hollow out the scye about ½ or ¾ inch, either at front and back or all round,

as it is seldom looked upon as a detriment for a breast to be large in the scye, and as long as sleeves are not added, we do not know there are any defects likely to arise from it. A button stand must be added all down the front, according to the style desired, ¾ of an inch being the amount usually allowed for an ordinary S.B. The length is obtained in the same way as described with the next system. In practice we have found this to work admirably, so can recommend it with confidence as being simple, reliable and quick. It, however, takes more of the practical than the scientific phase of cutting, so that it will be desirable for us to give the system for producing vests independently of the coat.

The Vest System.
Diagrams 57 and 58. Figure 31.

Draw line O 17. O 3 is ⅙ , raise point ¾, ¼ this quantity, O 9 is the depth of scye as taken. Draw line at right angles to this, hollow back seam at 17, 1½ inch., and mark off from back seam to 10½, 1½ inches more than chest measure, and come back from it ½ an inch less than the cross-chest measure taken; sweep from this point by a quarter of an inch less than the front shoulder less the width of back neck, and also from the front at 19½ by ¾ of an inch more than this quantity. Make point 3½ on back to taste, in this case ½ an inch less than ⅓ , O 9, and square across to 6½ ½ an inch less than the width of back, which in the absence of a measure may be fixed by making the width of shoulder seam ½ inch more than a fourth of breast; *i.e.*, the half breast. Now draw the shoulder seam of back and then measure across from 9 in the direction of shoulder seam, and whatever the back measures, deduct from the over-shoulder measure, and sweep by the remainder, less a quarter of an inch from a point 1½ inches above 12, but bringing the tape down to 12. Make the width of front shoulder a trifle less than the width of back and draw scye as shown. Make the width of back ½ the breast and ¾ of an inch, and the waist ½ waist and ¾ of an inch. Now square down from 9¾, and hollow 1 inch to find the side-seam of forepart and make the width of front at waist ½ waist and ¾ of an inch, and shape the underarm seam as shown by this arrangement the forepart will overlap the back for large waists. Special attention should be given to the spring over the hips as many vests are defective in this point. The lengths may now be marked for the opening and bottom, allowing ½ an inch extra for opening and 1 inch to the full length as per the measure taken, which allowances are for the amount consumed in the various seams. The height of gorge may be made ⅙ below the neck point, or higher or lower according to taste, and if anywhere near that point, it may be made a pivot by which to sweep for the side length from the bottom, as at 26, raising the side ½ inch above sweep; the back may be pointed upwards at bottom as shown, or arranged to taste. There is also another point which may be arranged either to taste or to get a large vest out of a small quantity of cloth, that is the underarm seam, and although the position allotted is perhaps the most suitable, yet the fronts may be made wider or narrower as the cutter wishes, the only point being that whatever is taken off the front must be added on the back, so that the combined widths of back and forepart measure 1½ inches over breast and waist from the centre of back to the centre of front at the respec-

tive parts. The pockets should be put as nearly as possible at the hollow of the waist, and we have found it a very good plan to come up 5 inches from the bottom for all ordinary length vests, to find the top of the front edge of the welt, which should measure about 5 inches long and ¾ or ⅞ wide. The watch pocket is put in slightly on the slant, its position not being a very vital matter, but it should be arranged for the back end to be slightly in front of the scye and about 2 inches or so below its level. A watch pocket welt should never measure less than 3½ inches long by ¾ wide; watches do not vary in size in accordance with the age or size of the wearer, so that it is quite necessary these should be made large enough to take a good-sized watch. There has been a good many dodges put forward at various times for the protection of watches from thieves, and we think amongst the best is the method of leaving the seam of the welt open wide enough to put the guard through; it will then be an impossibility for pickpockets to steal the watch. The buckle and strap should be put on at the hollow of waist, and we always prefer these to come into the sideseam and then fastened again to the back about one-third of the way across. In making, a pleat should be left through the front shoulder of the lining and the facing put on very tight at the bottom corner in order to make it curl inwards to the figure nicely, and the facing basted to the canvas. When the customer is very full over the hips it is frequently an advantage to leave slits at the side. The customer's wishes should be carefully studied in every detail, and prominent amongst these we must mention the guard-hole, as they get accustomed to wearing the chain in a certain position, and if the new vest is different to the old the change is most probably objected to. Many people

have a great objection to changes such as these; in fact, we think it may be traced to the inborn conservatism of the human race, for if you can only produce a garment to fit as easy and suit the wearer as well as the old one you are sure to please him. As will be seen, this diagram is finished in the step collar style, a collar being cut on the same lines as laid down for a coat but of course narrower. This is undoubtedly the leading style, but as represented here is specially suitable for a tweed, the edges being stitched. It may be as well, perhaps, to note that if thought desirable the scye may be enlarged to any reasonable extent without detriment.

We now come to the

French or No-collar Vest.
Diagram 58. Figure 32.

This is a very general favourite for boys' wear, and frequently worn with the Eton jacket. It is a very neat style, and is very popular at the present time. It is thinner round the neck, so that there is something to commend it. As will be noticed, this is arranged for bound edges, and, therefore, as there will not be any seam taken off the edges, it will not be necessary to allow on so much in front, and consequently only allow ½ an inch of button-stand. The only point of variation in the method of cutting is to fill up the neck as shown, to the extent of the height of collar-stand required by the customer, and leave a notch taken out to the hollowest part of gorge to which a collar band is sewn to come round the back neck. It will be noticed a small amount of spring is left at this notch; the purpose of this is to provide the necessary ease required by the neck at that part. This, although the only special feature in a no-collar vest, is a rather important one, and should never be overlooked, or the vest will slip away from the neck all round. As will

be seen, the welts are bound round the end, a plan that should always be adopted when high-class productions are aimed at as it gives a very much superior finish to the whole garment, and as the difference in time occupied between the two methods is so small, it should never be permitted to come into competition with the effects produced by the superior finish on the whole garment. Although only a small matter, yet to put in these details we can excel and produce results which will not only give us a reputation for excellence of workmanship, but help to raise the status of tailoring. As soon as each individual member of the craft realizes the fact that he is directly responsible for the elevation of tailoring, so soon shall we advance and place the profession on a footing second to none.

The Step-stand Vest.
Diagram 66. Figure 38.

This is cut precisely the same as the no-collar vest, the step being produced by a notch taken out, as shown, in whatever position deemed the most effective, the other part of the neck being kept, if anything, rather straighter. This is the style in which the majority of these are made, but, of course, they can be, and often are, produced by cutting the gorge down as for a step collar, and sewing on a collar forming the step at the end in the position desired.

This is a very simple style, yet it is astonishing how much difference a little taste makes in the position and shape of the notch.

The New Roll Collar.
Diagram 60. Figure 34.

This is a new style, and one that has a very dressy appearance, it is cut in just the shape it is desired when finished, and the collar stand being cut in one with the vest as described for the no-collar, and a band put in at the notch to go round the back neck, the collar for this is cut exactly the same shape as forepart, and is merely laid on. The method, perhaps, will be more readily gathered, if we refer to the fly of a pair of trousers, as an illustration of how this is done. These novelties are very good to teach the student how various effects are produced, rather than as standard styles, and as this is too extreme for that, we give it for the two-fold purpose of illustrating present fashion, as well as how to produce this effect. No-collar vests are sometimes cut with the opening above the top button cut the in same way, but these and other novelties are only made so casually, that they hardly demand a place in such a work as this, as although youths are always on the alert for something fresh, yet their parents have to be consulted in this matter, and they always object to anything of an extreme character, justly judging that the acme of good taste is to have every garment harmonizing with each other to such an extent, that it would be difficult to say any part of the costume was conspicuous.

The Roll Collar.
Diagram 61. Figure 36.

This is produced by precisely the same diagram as the step collar, in fact, the only variation being that the collar is brought to the end of the lapel, and formed into a graceful turn. This style of vest is the one that perhaps more than any other is worn with the Eton Jacket, although the no-collar vest would run it close for this. It is also the Groom's Livery Vest, besides being frequently worn on ordinary occasions. The edges in this diagram are left bluff, that style being the general rule for Livery, and when black cloth was used for Eton Jackets, it was customary to leave it bluff

for that also, but as the garments are so seldom made from this material now, black Worsted and Vicuna having superseded it, the mode of finishing the edges have varied in like manner, so that the Worsteds are usually bound and the Vicunas and soft Wools stitched or corded. The cutter who knows his business will note which are the most effective finishes for the various materials, and so produce the best results in each garment. These are some of the points where the art comes in, and as we claim to be artists, we should know how the best effect on each individual customer can be produced from a garment of a given material, and if in our opinion the material is unsuitable, such as would be the case if a prominent stripe is selected for a suit for a tall thin youth, or a large check for a stout one; it then becomes our duty to suggest other patterns, and if we do it in a judicious manner, customers will readily listen to the claims of art, it being their aim, as well as ours for them, to clothe in such garments as will make them appear to the best advantage.

The Dress Vest.
Diagram 62. Figure 35.

This is cut in precisely the same way as described for the no-collar, namely the gorge filled up to the extent of about $\frac{5}{8}$ of an inch, or equal to the height of the collar stand, and the front hollowed out as shown, It is a difficult matter to make them too hollow at the lower part. At the same time it must be the aim of the cutter to retain a harmonious run or curve with the opposite side, still the one great point is to keep it well hollow at the bottom. It is also advisable as producing a better effect, if it is slightly rounded near the top at 13¼, or midway between the neck point and the level of scye; this forms a more artistic

curve than if kept very hollow all the way up, and at the same time helps to keep it snug to the figure at that part. Although it is highly essential to keep it close-fitting at the hollow, yet we do not find it necessary to do more than steady it. V's are decidedly objectionable, as producing far too short a front edge, and making the garment stand away at the bottom, a defect Dress Vests seem to be specially liable to. The collar is cut by the forepart, and it is just as well to cut these a trifle more hollow, so as to throw a little more ease on the outside edge, as if this is at all contracted it is liable to turn outwards and show the collar lining. The outside collar is made to just turn over the crease edge, say ½ an inch, and the lining felled to it. Our diagram illustrates the style in which they are generally finished, as well as the amount of opening. There are usually three buttons only and two pockets, the welts for which are rather lighter than usual, being from ⅝ to ¾. As will be seen, the edges are traced with narrow Russia braid, and again behind that is a fancy tracing braid, which produces a very nice effect. In the bottom corner a flower is embroidered in black silk. This, however, is only adopted occasionally, and by such young gentlemen who are desirous of having something exceptionally stylish. These are generally made from the same material as the coat, and when not so, are either white Marcella or Pique. or a white or fancy Silk, Moiré, or Watered Silk is very popular at present, and amongst the novelties in Dress Vests this season, we noted many of this material. There have also been a large number made for gentlemen who may be looked upon as leaders of the fashion of the D.B. style, cut in precisely the same manner as this, but with a 1¾ to 2¼ button stand allowed on, which being pointed slightly upwards comes under the roll; this is terminated in ex-

actly the same manner as on this diagram. Others, again, have had the corners cut away from the bottom hole to about 4 inches across the bottom, producing rather a light effect. Some may think we have made this diagram to open rather low, but such is not the case, it being a very usual custom with many firms to cut them quite ½ inches lower than illustrated. One very important point must be noted in connection with Dress Vests, and that is, that they do not come below the strap of the coat; with this end in view, it should always be tried on at the same time as the coat, as any discrepancy at this part is very unsightly, and evidences a great amount of carelessness, or a want of technical knowledge, both of which are serious faults in one whose profession it is to be fully acquainted with every detail of how all kinds of clothing should appear when on the figure, and in fact have an ideal in their minds of what the finished garment should be.

When these Vests are made from white material, it is the general rule to put eyelets for the buttons to be fastened with split rings through their shanks, so that they can be removed when it is required to be washed; for the same purpose the buckle is put on at the back with a hole and button, so as to avoid discoloration of the Vest by its possible rusting. The old style of Dress Vest, which is now seldom seen except for livery servants, is cut in the same method as diagram 51, but of course to roll much lower, the same principles, however, are involved, and all the parts produced as therein described. The only point worth noting is, that whilst a heavy roll looks clumsy, yet the opposite extreme must be avoided, and to do so it will be found necessary to cut on a little *"belly"* to the lapel. We now come to

D.B. Vest,
Figure 37,

That garment being decidedly popular at the present time, the only actual variation in cut being the addition of a lapel, or, putting it in other words, a very wide button stand, the lowering of the gorge being a point which may or may not be done, and is guided by the height the step is desired. If it is required to have the Vest to fasten up to the throat, it will be necessary to cut the lapel an exact counterpart of the forepart, which may be done by creasing or folding it down the breast line, and cutting that part off which comes over the breast line; this will form the V at the neck, and this is the only plan of getting it to fit well up at the neck and clean over the breast; any reduction in the size of this will show itself in a corresponding surplus length on the outer edge. As will be seen in the diagram, only a very small V is taken out at this part, as when the lapel rolls over as illustrated, a little extra length is needed to go over the round of breast; the immediate result of this V is to shorten the outside length of lapel. The width of lapel is quite a matter of taste, and is fixed in this instance at 1¾ at bottom, 2¼ at top, and 2¾ in the widest part. The proper method of fixing the position of the buttons, is to mark where the eye of the hole will come, and then sweep from it by making a pivot at any point on the breast line, such as X at bottom. Now repeat the operation by the X or lapel, which as will be seen is on the breast line, and where these arcs cross each other gives the exact position of the buttons, and ensures them being on the same level as the holes, and just as far behind the breast line as the eye of the hole is in front. This is a simple and reliable method, which we have no doubt will be appreciated now these Vests have become

popular, and as the same principle applies to all D.B. garments, it will give a good guide for the fixing the exact position of the buttons on such. In making, it is often customary to cut away that part of the lapel beyond the crease row, and merely leaving on a little above the end of lapel, as per dash line; this of course is more generally practiced on the score of economy, but at the same time it gives a thinner lapel, though one that cannot be worked up so well. This, however, is not of so much importance as with a coat, it being the general plan to fasten the top corner down to the forepart, either by a secret stitch or a button at that part. A tommy button is put to secure the under part in position, and prevent it riding up and making the crease edge appear loose. The pockets are put in about the same position as for other styles, the only difference being that they are rather more to the side, which is necessitated by the overlap. The last style of Vest we shall notice at this part is

The Sleeve Vest.
Diagram 64. Figure 38,

And although not so often worn by youths, yet as it forms a class by itself, we should have left our work incomplete if it had not been included. The only variation necessary is in the scye section which should be made to come as close up to the natural juncture of the arm and body as possible, as no sleeves fit as well as those that are cut for a scye in such a position, hence it will be seen the scye is raised a ¼ and which extends all round the scye, with the exception of at B, whilst it is increased to ⅜ or ½ an inch at the shoulder, so that the back should measure one-fifth breast from C to D; the sleeve is then produced in the manner previously described for Jackets, but as there are one or two variations, we will repeat

Measure across from back at A to front of scye at B, and deduct the width of back as at CD, the remainder is used to find the distance O 3½. Now mark the front pitch of the sleeve at ¾ of an inch above the level of scye and the hindarm to taste, and apply the square with the arms as at B resting on the pattern in the position the sleeve is desired to hang from the scye, this may be altered by shifting the square round, but still keeping either arm at the pitches. The more forward the sleeve is desired to hang, the greater the distance that shows itself at B, and *vice versa*. Having obtained this quantity, apply it to the sleeve by coming up as from 3½ to ½ now measure across the distance between the two pitches, with the back placed in a closing position at the shoulder, and make ½ to 8½ agree with this quantity, never less but rather more, as many of the defects in the fitting of sleeve vests arises from the fact of the sleeves being too small. 4½ is midway between O and 8½ and the sleeve head shaped by these points, now measure the distance between the two pitches for the underside, and apply this measure across from 3½ to 7½. The underside of sleeve should not be hollowed out below 3½, in fact it should be rather rounded than hollowed for the undersleeve, for although this undoubtedly detracts from the cleanness of fit at that part, yet it produces ease, and allows the arms to be lifted without feeling a drag on the arm, and as the sleeve vest is fastened all the way down the front, any lack of ease in this direction would produce a considerable strain, and if the vest did not come moderately close up in the scye, the whole vest would be raised bodily. It is a very great mistake to think that ease in the scye (of a sleeved vest at any rate) can be produced by a deep scye, for in the movement of the arms, such as would take place in the wear of a sleeve vest, a deep scye would produce anything but ease, and we should expect to find either the sewing or the material go at that part.

The hind arm of elbow should be got by drawing a line at right angle from ½ to 8½, and measuring forward for the size of sleeve, hollowing the elbow in front, to the amount it is desired to reduce, which in this case is 1¾. The cuff is got in just the opposite way, viz., by squaring down on the other side of sleeve, and making the forearm at cuff to rest on this line, and measuring from it to find the width of cuff. The run of the cuff is got by drawing it at right angles to the elbow and cuff, whilst the lengths are of course fixed by the measure taken, plus the three seams consumed.

The one great point to be avoided in a sleeve vest, is a small sleeve head, far away better have too much sleeve head than not enough. In making, the sleeves are generally finished with a hole and button at the cuff, and the lining of the sleeves are much better sewn separately to the oufside, and flash-basted at both seams and put in rather long.

This, we think, concludes our remarks on vests, and from which we think the intelligent cutter should be able to produce any kind of vest, which although only an under-garment, and one that does not force its defects prominently before our notice, yet is well worthy our careful consideration, and is just that garment which has more latitude allowed it in fancy or artistic designs, so that it becomes the duty of every cutter who has the trade at heart to give it his most careful study.

The number of buttons usually put up the front of a youth's vest varies from five to six, six or seven being plenty for the full size garment. The buttons on a vest often form its special feature, and much taste may be displayed in the number and kind used.

Trousers

We now come to deal with trousers, and doing so we feel the immense importance of the subject, and the very great difficulties which stand in the way before we can possibly attain perfection, so much so that we are more than ever convinced a trouser which shall fit without a wrinkle or crease in any of the various positions the legs may assume in conjunction with the body is a practicable impossibility, yet these are the garments many expect, and it is nothing to be surprised at if they are disappointed. To such we hold out no hopes, our endeavours will rather be to place such principles as will enable the intelligent cutter to distinguish what causes produce given effects, and to so apply them as to reduce the defects in trousers to a minimum. It may interest many of the "perfection seeking class" to examine their own body minus the clothing in a looking glass, and by placing themselves in a variety of positions to see how the skin wrinkles and creases and forms folds of surplus length and width; or if they wish something easier, let them screw up their hand in such a position as would be done if dipping up water, and then look at its creases and folds, or, still further, look at the knuckles and see the surplus skin forms itself in ridges on them; what is the purpose of it all but to allow of certain movements. Bend the knuckles or open the palm there is no surplus material there then; just so is it with trousers, and what is the production of our great Creator would hardly be called a misfit, a flaw or a blemish, but rather looked upon as an illustration of the perfection of His work, and yet when we apply the same principle to the production of trousers and produce identical effects with material far away less elastic

than the skin, the surplus length which allows for variation in position is looked upon by some as a defect. How many tailors are there who are trying every fresh system and all sorts of dodges to get rid of the creases at the back of thighs just directly under the ball of the seat? Yet if the maker of the system knows his business he would make a special arrangement in the working of his system which would produce just that surplus length at that part to enable the wearer to sit down or stoop, and yet this is productive of these very folds, and we should advise them to relinquish such a "Will o' the wisp" chase, for if they got what they wanted they would find it far from what they expected, and that other and far more serious faults would be apparent at other parts if these were absent.

Again there is no system so perfect in its application but requires departing from for certain forms of figures, and the method we are about to elucidate is no exception. Space however will prevent our dealing with any other than the upright well-formed figure so refer our readers to the Federation Prize essay on trousers cutting or the new work on Livery Garments for our views on the deviations necessary for the various abnormalities to be met with in daily practice, such as corpulent and thin waists, knock knees, bow legs, and many other irregularities in form and position. The system as laid down in these, although practically the same in effect is not exactly the same as in the above work, the reason for the few alterations made will be fully explained when we come to it. Preparatory to this it will be as well to look at those principles or constituent parts which govern the fit and go to make up a pair of trousers. It is needless

to remark they consists of a body and two legs, yet it is in the relation the one bears to the other that many of the defects may be traced, for it must always be remembered that the legs of the trousers are forced to follow the legs of the wearer except to the small scope allowed by their width, and just as they are made to swing in or out, or in other words are open or close, will there be cleanness about the fork or surplus material there. Then again there is another factor to the fitting of trousers, and one which is often overlooked, viz., the harmony of the parts, that is the undersides being cut the same in the balance as the topsides, and we are of opinion very few indeed are to be found fully cognisant of the result that would be produced by letting the undersides pass up or down at the sideseams. We all know it affects the hang of the sideseam, but it does not end there, and if those who are striving after knowledge on this topic will make the experiment, we think they will learn much from it.

The body part

Is precisely the same as is contained in the plaid Kilt, or any garment which wraps right round independently of the legs. For convenience's sake we divide it into top and undersides, and there is of course no actual necessity for a sideseam in this, it only asserts its claims when the legs are added. If we were going to cut a perfectly close-fitting garment without any division of the legs, it would be necessary for us to allow a certain amount for ease over and above the consumption of seams for which of course we should allow the usual ¼ inch. It is rather an interesting, and certainly a very instructive experiment, to test how much the body expands at the seat when sitting, and especially to those who have never thought why so much more was allowed over the measures of the seat than

was consumed by the seams. In teaching, we always make it a practice to give a reason for all we do; possibly some are more apparent than others, if so, this is one of the most so, for we find that the difference between a measure taken fairly close round the seat, just about the hip bone, is at least 1½ or 2 inches smaller than if taken with the same degree of tightness when sitting, hence the necessity of allowing 1 inch or thereabouts for ease, besides the ¼ inch for every seam. At the waist there is no expansion such as this to be provided for, so that the allowance for seams is sufficient at that part. An interesting question, however, comes in at this juncture, viz., at what part should this inch of ease be placed? Some allow it on the back seam and produce a very round seat seam, others allow it on the side seam. It has been our custom, however, to place it midway, which is done by taking out a 1 inch fish at about the middle, or a trifle nearer the sideseam of undersides, see

Diagram 68.

This method distributes the size more equally over the seat, and we have always found it to produce satisfactory results. However, we have no wish to say it is the only spot for it, for although the figure increases in width when sitting, yet undoubtedly the increase takes place at the back, so that although we have every confidence in the plan we have laid down as being the most satisfactory, and as far as we can see in accordance with the development of the figure when sitting, yet if our readers think it should be put on the seat seam in the form of a round at S, in diagram 57, they may do so, but in doing so they must not reduce the angle from the fork-point to the top of sideseam or undersides, so that the V will be taken as it were from the seat seam at back. We only mention this so as to fully explain principles, and why patterns, apparently so very different in outline, may both fit very nearly the same.

The Fork.

This is undoubtedly that part which joins the forepart to the undersides through the legs, and although it is very closely allied to seat angle, yet it is a totally distinct quantity and one which serves a different purpose. In the Federation Prize Essay, this quantity was obtained by taking the tight thigh undress side and treating the thigh as a circle, taking the diameter of it. It has occurred to us this is scarcely logical, and although it has been found to operate in the most satisfactory manner in thousands of cases, yet we think this will be, if possible, an improvement; at any rate it will be a more logical treatment of it, and with the view of making this as plain as possible, we have prepared

Diagram 71,

Which shows the gluteal and femoral sections of the body in their relative positions to each other, or, speaking in easier language, the seat and thighs. The thigh although being slightly elliptical, yet is not sufficiently so to demand any variation of the treatment from a circle, and as we undoubtedly have to deal more with circumference than diameter in connection with this, we have come to the conclusion that ¼ of the circumference of the tight thigh, plus the allowance for dress, (which may be easily determined by taking the measures of both thighs at the same degree of closeness), will give us as nearly as possible the correct amount of fork. This will in most cases come to exactly the same as the diameter, as both bear a fixed relation to the circumference, the allowance for dress varying from ¾ to 1½ inches. Let us take as an example a lad with a 32 seat, and 19 thigh; the diameter would be 6, whilst ¼ would be 4¾

plus 1¼ equals 6. Some may consider 1¼ excessive for dress allowance, but we think not, as it is the universal custom to put whatever surplus shirt there may be at that part on the dress side; but if the measurement should prove 1 inch to be sufficient, well, the difference is then only ¼ inch, and we are of opinion the present quantity would be the most correct. Turning to the diagram, F to G shows the diameter, and D to E the part allotted to the fork with the addition of the dress at that side. It will be noticed from this diagram the ball of the seat extends backwards beyond the thigh, as illustrated from G to H; this is what necessitates a certain amount of SEAT ANGLE, coupled with the necessity for an allowance for stooping, sitting and so on. The former will require a 1 inch wedge, and the latter about 2 more, and making in all about 3 inches, this seat angle may be looked upon as a wedge let in the trousers directly above the thighs, and is shown on diagram 68, and bounded by 3, 9, 12. If we make a mark on the body just on the round of the seat, and another just about mid-thighs, and measure the distance between these in an upright or standing position, and again, with the body bent as when in the act of stooping or sitting. We shall find the distance between the two marks on the skin has increased at least 4 or 5 inches. This shows the necessity for sitting down room, or to use the more technical term, "seat angle". When the body is so bent, there is no surplus length at top of thighs, but there is decidedly too much material in the lap; this, however, vanishes, when the figure stands upright, and the wrinkles and folds appear at the bottom of seat. That this is necessary will be apparent to all, and it is the direct results of these allowances for sitting, stooping, &c. Of course, if a gentleman desired a pair of trousers *only to walk in,* and we believe such demands are occasionally made, this seat angle might be reduced, to say, 1 inch, and the amount for ease almost, if not entirely dispensed with; but it is not everyone who will have special trousers for each exercise he may take, hence the necessity for our producing garments that shall meet the general wants, and be as free from defects as possible. We trust that this will be sufficient to show that it is quite possible to produce a "Fashion Plate fit" on anyone, so long as they remain in one position, but as to the fit being perfection in every position, the thing is an impossibility and should never be expected.

We now come to deal with another point in connection with trousers cutting, and that is: which is the most reliable measure to use as a factor in finding the fork quantity, the thigh or the seat? Some assert one and some the other, whilst others again look upon it as immaterial. Dr. Wampen is of this latter class, giving it as his opinion there are counteracting influences at work which almost nullify the variations which would be produced by either plan. However, we prefer

The Thigh Measure

For this purpose, and our reasons for doing so are as follows; by a reference to figure 1, it will be seen that the thigh bone is one of those parts of the human framework, the skeleton, which always remains near the surface of the skin, and that any abnormal development of the thighs would take place at the inside of the leg. A reference to the figure will show that about three-fourths of the flesh of the thigh is on the inside of bone, and consequently it increases or diminishes at that part, and as it does so it increases or decreases the distance between the legs at the crutch B, diagram 71, and at 10, figure 1. This, archway is termed the cocyxial quantity. Now this has nothing to do with fork, but rather the division of the width ot the leg, so that it is hollower or straighter according as it increases or diminishes, so that whenever the thigh is small, the fork requires to be less, but the stride more, and *vice versa*. Of course it is only in extreme cases the difference between the two methods are seen, and as we believe in such the thigh measure would give the most accurate results, we have adopted it, looking upon it as occupying the same relation to trouser cutting that the shoulder measure does to coat cutting, in fact the parts are very similar in their developments of growth, for just as the line or the top of the shoulder at 1 x, figure 1, always remains at the surface of the skin, and any development of size takes place at the bottom, so does the thigh bone 6 x figure 1, remain at the surface, and the flesh develop itself on the innerside of thigh. This will be of much service to us in our consideration of fixing the centre of leg, so as to obtain a reliable starting point from which to equally distribute the width desired in the legs. This undoubtedly should be so arranged as to come at F and G, and our method of finding this is ⅛ of the tight thigh as shown on Diagram 71, F to D, plus half the cocyxial quantity as at B, and which we have already pointed out increases or diminishes in opposite directions to the relative size of thigh and seat. At the same time, it is as well we should point out that we think there is very little to choose between this method and taking one-sixth of the half seat, as in the larger number of cases it will be found they exactly agree, for if the seat is large in relation to the thigh, the cocyxial quantity would be increased, and so make up what the division of the small thigh was lacking, to make it agree with the division of the seat, so that

practically either method would produce the same result, and be equally correct, hence the division of width line can either be found by ⅛ tight undress thigh, plus half distance the legs are apart at crutch, or ⅙ of the half seat. Some may prefer the seat measure for this on account of the difficulty in obtaining the cocyxial quantity, if not we should by all means advise them to use it, they will find it quite reliable.

The closing and fly seam of the trousers must occupy the position A C when on the body, and no matter how cut in relation to the other parts, they will still retain this position. Having thus looked at the principles which govern the fit of trousers, we will proceed to lay down.

The Trousers System.

And begin with the forepart, diagram 67. Line O 45 is the edge of the cloth, on which mark off the length of side from O to 45, and back from 45 to 12 the length of leg. Now square across from 12, and make 12 to 9¼ seat, and draw a line up at right angles to find fly line, and square the top of front by this, the natural waist line 9, 1, 2, may be made ¼ seat and 1 inch, up from line 12, 9. In the absence of a measure having been taken for this, and mark off ¼ waist and two seams equal ½ inch, and draw sideseam, springing it out above this line, and curving it out to E, which may be fixed at rather less than ⅛ seat above 12, that being the position of the hip bone, see figure 1, 6 x, and is the most prominent point at the side of trousers. From 9 to 12¼ is half the fork, which quantity is found by taking ¼ tight thigh, and adding on the difference between the two thighs, which may be fixed at from 1 to 1½ inches, or found by measures taken at that part; thus: 38 seat, 22 and 23½ thigh, ¼ thigh, 5½, plus the difference 1½ equal 7, the half of which would be 3½. From 9 measure out to 1¾ rather more than half the distance 9, 12¼, and draw fork by a graceful deadened curve, always avoiding making it too hollow, and starting ⅙ seat up from point 9. The division of width line at 6 is fixed at ⅓ thigh and half the cocyxial quantity, (½ an inch for proportion), or by one-sixth of the half seat. It is in the angle at which this is drawn, which produces the open or close style of cut. For ordinary figures who require their trousers to fit in a natural position, this line may be drawn at right angles to 12, 12¼, bringing it more to the side at bottom for easy or open-cut trousers, or more to the leg for the close cut, always retaining point 6 in the same position. Having fixed the position of line 6, we divide the width it is desired to have the legs equally on each side at the knee, plus a seam equal ¼ inch, (the position of the knee may generally be fixed at 2 inches above the half of the leg measure). The width at bottom may then be dealt with in the same manner, with the exception that the width at inside of leg is made ½ inch small, so as to bring the legseam rather more forward; the bottoms should be slightly hollowed at 6, making the hollowest part 1 inch nearer the sideseam than 6. One of the new make of trouser sticks is of great advantage to draught the seams of trousers, by keeping them to a graceful curve, at the same time making the operation simple and more expeditious.

The Underside.

Having cut out the topsides, we place them in such a position on the cloth, as will allow the centre of legs to run with a stripe, if possible. Mark round the fork and make up the size at bottom by adding on at leg seam what was omitted from the topside and round the bottom as shown. Now come up from 9, 3 inches, for boys, this may be made $\frac{1}{12}$ seat. Place the square on a line drawn from 12 to this point, and draw the seat seam at right angles to this, and make it form one continuous run with the fork. Now measure across from S to E in the manner shown by tape on diagram 68, and whatever that measures, place it on A of undersides, and measure forward to T the seat measure and 2 inches, (1 inch for seams, the other inch for allowance for the expansion of the body when sitting and stooping). It will be noticed that A is above point S, and taken across the seat in a slanting direction. The reason for this is, that as the seat angle or the 3 inches inserted from 9 upwards drops down in surplus length when on the figure, as the seat seam must come up the centre. A then comes opposite S, hence the necessity for bringing A the amount of seat angle above S, thus the combined size of seat, measures 2 inches more than the half-seat. Now make the knee at sideseam a pivot to sweep from the top of topsides to find the correct length of sideseam of underside. Having done this, measure across the size of waist. of topsides and apply the tape as shown, and making the combined size of top and undersides the half waist and seams, or if a fish is taken out, which we always advise when possible, allow another inch for the fish and two seams, thus making in all 2½ inches over the half waist; now place the square on the seat seam, and draw a line from this point up to 2¼ so that the undersides are still the amount of seat angle longer than the topsides, at the closing seam, so that allowing the seat angle to drop, as it undoubtedly will, when on, the top of underside will come on the same level as the top of the fronts. If it is desired to wear braces, it will be necessary to add on 1½ inches at 2 from the closing seam, if allowance has been made for a fish being taken out, proceed to mark it, but keep it well away

from the sideseam, and landing the fulness at that part where judgment shows it is most required, a trifle further back than illustrated in these diagrams will be better than further forward. The sideseam may now be drawn from the points obtained, and if the thighs are desired to be particularly close-fitting, it may be hollowed in there a trifle. The only remaining operation is

The taking out of the Dress,
Diagram 67.

Make from 8 to 9 the difference between the two thigh measures; 11¼, 12¼ is also fixed in the same way. Sweep from knee to avoid making the undress side any shorter, and take out the dress from ¼ the seat up. In the Federation Prize Essay, we pointed out this took away the allowance made for the cocyxial quantity, but at the same time pointed out the dress occupied this position, so that it is quite unnecessary for us to say any more on this topic, as doubtless most of my readers will have procured that work, if not they will find in it much food for thought. We have often been asked to arrange this system to work with a division of the seat, as many have no opportunity to take their own measures, and consequently have to take the proportionate thigh, and this practically reduces it to a seat measure method, we give the necessary information with pleasure. Make 12 to 6 ⅓ seat, 12 to 9½ and 12 to 12¼ a trifle over ⅔ seat, say ¼ inch over, and take out the dress as previously described, of one-twelfth of the half seat. There is another point which has formed the subject of correspondence, and that is the apparent waste of material down the sideseam, and if the side at bottom could not be brought close to 45. Of course it can, but in doing so you are slightly twisting the pattern on the legs, and the query is, whether the 1½ inches that comes off the side is of more value than the pattern running with the leg. We do not think it is, hence our reason for fixing a method which will produce the highest result, still, we know there are occasions when every inch of cloth is of value. Then point 6 may be made ¼ the size of bottom desired, plus seams, and 12, 6 ⅓ seat, all the other lines being squared from it. The method is fully illustrated in the new work on Livery Garments. However, it is a plan which detracts from the style and effect of a good-fitting garment, and should only be resorted to under exceptional circumstances. The only other point we will notice in the trouser system, is the position of the buttons, we are of opinion the front button should stand nearly ¼ waist, *i.e.*, ⅛ total waist from the fly seam, and the next one 3½ or 3¾ from it, whilst the back one should not be more than 2 inches from closing seam at back. There are many other phases of this most important subject, which we should be only too pleased to discuss, but having dealt with them in the work previously mentioned, we should be only swelling the bulk of the present volume, and thereby adding to its cost unnecessarily, if we repeated them, so must refer our readers to that book for a further elucidation of the principles we have set down. We will only further note the peculiarities of those styles which are worn by boys and youths, and we suppose there is no style of nether garment which has grown more rapidly in popularity, than

Knickerbockers & Knickerbocker Breeches
Diagrams 69 & 70. Figure 9.

There is no variation in the body parts of these, unless they are made very loose fitting at the thighs when the seat follows suit. The special features in these are to allow sufficient length to form the bag over arrangement at knee. 3 inches is a minimum of surplus length beyond the actual measure to the point at which it is desired they shall terminate on the leg; 4 inches is preferable for this. They should be made loose, and in the absence of any better guide, 2 inches over the half seat may be taken as the present fashion width, some have them wider than this, but this is a medium style which may be safely followed. Knickers are sometimes finished merely with a piece of elastic put in the hem at bottom, and at others are put into a band, in which case the larger amount of fulness should be placed in front. Some firms reduce the size of knees, by fishes, which is specially suitable when the material is very thick, but in thin substance the effect is much better when it is fulled into a garter or elastic. Knickerbocker Breeches are produced exactly the same, but have a band sewn in at the bottom 3½ or 4 inches wide, and finished with three holes and buttons, the top button coming in the small just below the knee, in order to make them fit clean and give the desired ease for the calf of leg. Diagram 70 is very suitable, it is produced by taking a strip of paper, cutting it at ¼ up to 10, and letting it overlap about ⅜, and thus producing the hollow and tightness at bottom, and the round at top. The reverse operation at 10, viz., cut from 10 to ½ and open half an inch, which produces the opposite result, viz., round edge at bottom and hollow at top. This band is frequently made of drab Devon, and made up very firm, being frequently lined with canvas, the object being to combine the support of breeches with the comfort of knickerbockers. We do not think it is necessary for us to repeat how to find the various points, as that has already been fully dealt with, suffice it to say, they are found in precisely the same manner as described for trousers, diagrams 67 and 68, and although the dress is not shown in

this and succeeding diagrams, yet it may be taken from them all, following the directions given under that head.

Shorts.
Diagram 72. Figure 19.

These are extensively used by boys when at school, and may be best explained as short trousers. We have arranged them without any fish out of the undersides; for two reasons; the first to show how this was arranged, the second to call attention to the fact that Eton trousers should always be cut so, as it is always advisable to avoid having anything which would give the impression of piecing. This is arranged by hollowing the waist at back another ¾ inch inside seat seam, making up the size of waist at side and allowing 1 inch for seams only. Besides the garments usually worn by boys for ordinary wear, there are those which are worn for racing and athletic performances, these are generally cut shorter in the legs, and the waist large enough to pull up over the hip and fasten with a drawing string round the waist, and consequently the button front is unnecessary. To cut these the sideseam may be drawn straight up from the bottom and hips, as a little surplus width at the waist is no detriment. We now come to

Cycling Breeches.
Diagram 73. Figure 6.

The special feature to be studied in these garments, is to allow sufficient angle and room in the seat to allow of the free action of the legs. The method we have adopted with the most satisfactory results is as follows: After fixing all the points by the same method as for trousers, recede the fronts ½ inch, and cut the topsides from 1 to 1¼ inches longer in the leg to allow for plenty of fulness being put over the knee,

and in dealing with the undersides, increase the seat angle 1 inch, and allow 1 inch of length from the fork line upwards, to allow of their being held on that much over the seat. They should be cut long enough to prevent their working up over the knee; and the bottom should be finished with a garter and buckle, which should be kept tight across the topside and held on slightly at back. Three or four buttons should be placed at the side, the top one being placed at the small, and the tack just below knee. As will be noticed the buttons are kept well at the side, a feature we have found to be in accordance with the wishes of the majority of cyclists. Two inches will be ample to allow over the seat measure, unless they are required very easy, when another half inch might be added; the shaded parts on the seat show the size seat piece generally put on outside, whilst the inside is lined with either flannel or chamois leather. The pockets for this style are generally put in cross, and we have occasionally omitted them in front and put in short seat pockets. These are details, however, which are best obtained from each individual customer, our experience going to prove this class of customers are rare fidgets, but know what they want.

Riding Breeches.
Diagram 74.

Many young gentlemen require garments of this class, especially those who may be regarded as the upper ten. As at present-worn they are very baggy at the thighs and close-fitting at the knee, whilst the buttons are brought decidedly forward. The working of the system for these is as follows: find all the points as for trousers, and then instead of squaring up at right angles on line 12 from 9, drop the square down to 13½ and get the fly line at right angles to 13½ 9; get the run of top by squaring from the

original fly line, and in dividing the width of legs at knee, make the topside ½ to 1 inch narrower at sideseam, this is done with the view of bringing the buttons forward. Allow 1 inch of extra length for fulling on beyond the actual measure and use care not to get the knees too large. As a general rule the knee can be fixed at 2 inches above the half leg, the small being 2 inches below the knee, and the calf about 3 inches below the small. Of course this is only the average, but as such it may be of use. In dealing with the undersides, the seat angle is drawn by using point 13½ in place of 12, see dot and dash line, and is the same in effect as if a 2 inch wedge were taken out from side at 12 to nothing at fork, 12¼. The SEAT is made up to measure and 3½ inches for the present baggy style, and any deficiency at the sides of top at knee made up at undersides as shown. 1 inch should be allowed for fulling on over the seat; the top of undersides finished as for trousers, a little extra length at back being no detriment for these. The tack is placed 1 inch below the knee, and the first button put at the small. The strappings at inside of leg are not always put on, although done so very frequently, and are either of leather or the same material as the breeches, and generally stitched in the manner illustrated to keep them in position. To these are frequently added

Continuations.
Diagram 76.

These are generally made from a thinner cloth, the seam is placed down the back; the method of draughting is very simple. Draw line O, 10; O to 7½ is half size of top, plus a seam; and 10, 5¾ is half the size of bottom, plus a seam. From O to 2¼ is ½ inch less than 6, 2¾ of the breeches, that being the actual centre of front, as most peoples' feet turn out to that extent. From 10 to

2¼ is the same amount which finds the one side, the other part being produced precisely the same at the back part; and the front, a button stand, say 1 inch less than 2¼ is from 10 and O. These are generally made up very thin, the buttons which should be very flat, put rather wide apart.

Leggings,
Diagram 75.

These are so generally used with breeches that we should be very remiss if we did not give a system for producing them. As at present worn they are very round at bottom, rather large, and the buttons arranged so as to come nearly over the centre of foot, 7 holes placed at equal distances, and, as will be seen, some distance from the bottom. A gentleman in ordering a pair of these from me, said, "I want these to have the same effect as a Newmarket boot, *i.e.*, a top boot with Devon tops". This so nearly expresses the ideal of leggings as worn at present, that no better illustration could be found to convey the correct idea to our readers. The system is as follows: Draw line O 14, hollow it ⅜ at ankle, and if the gentleman has fairly proportioned calves take out ¾ at top, and measure forward to 7½ the half size of top, plus seams, and the same at bottom, and draw a line down front; and, if any variation has to be made in the size of calf, make it at the back. Draw the top of legging at right angles to line 7½, 7½, and allow on the buttonholes in accordance with the position they are desired to take, remembering the front line of legging should come about half an inch to the side of the division of width line of breeches, for the reason previously given. If this is made more than sufficient for a button stand, reduce the smaller side as much as is beyond the front line, but leaving sufficient for a button stand. Well

round the bottoms away as shown in 1 and 2 from 7½ and this, will produce a legging as made in one of the most celebrated houses for this speciality in London. They are generally faced with the same material round the bottom and up the buttonhole side, the button stand being stayed with linen, jean or canvas. A loop is left at top to fasten them to the breeches and keep the leggings in place, as well as a loop being left behind (if the material is too thick or otherwise unsuitable for a buttonhole) to fasten to the calf button.

The white buckskin ties usually put on breeches at knee are intended to further help in keeping the leggings in place as well as relieving the strain, or allow it to be adjusted tighter or looser as desired, and should show just above the top of the leggings, or top boots if the latter are worn.

Pyjama Suit for Sleeping.
Plate 15. Diagram 77 and 78. Figure 39.

Each season brings these garments into increased popularity, so that now no hosier's stock is considered complete without them. They are a good deal worn by the better class of youth at public schools, and consequently we give them a place in this work. It is not necessary for us to consider wherein the advantage lies over the old style of night-shirt. Suffice it for us there is a demand for them, and if we wish to keep pace with the times we must be ready with the supply, or at any rate be competent to execute orders for such. They are made from Oxford shirting, flannel, silk, and such like materials, and are generally coloured, stripes and checks being more popular than self shades. As will readily be seen by the diagrams and figure, they are made very loose-fitting. The trousers are cut in precisely the same manner as just described, with the exception that they are cut with a

straight sideseam, so that, if desired, the seam may be omitted, which, we may say, is the plan more generally adopted; a straight sideseam is therefore, indispensable, so that after fixing the size at bottom and the size at seat, draw a straight line through these two points, the excess of width at the waist so produced being drawn in with a cord and tassel through a hem at the top. Having cut the top and underside pattern in this manner, it will be easy to lay it on the material with the sideseam joining as if it were one. The seams are generally sewn and felled over in the same way as usually done for a shirt, and the front is left open about nine or ten inches from the top, say to just below S, diagram 77. If the knees are required smaller, the only plan will be to reduce them at legseam, unless there is a sideseam, when the usual method may be followed.

The Jacket.
Diagram 78. Figure 39.

The various points for this are formed in the same manner as laid down for the Lounge, but as they are usually cut with a whole back, nothing is taken out at the hollow of waist; the sideseam is also drawn straight, and the forepart made to overlap the back ½ to 1½ inches, according to the amount of ease desired. They are usually made to button down the front, and a breast pocket is often added. The collar is of the stand type, made to the size of neck. The sleeves are made quite plain, and may be cut in the same way as shown in diagram 9; the only variation that may be made is to increase the size of elbow slightly. The style of trimming illustrated by our diagram is also a very popular one, and shows cords placed double across the breast, and finished at the end with a crow's foot, left long enough on the one side to loop, over button on the other. The seams are finished in the same manner as described for the trousers. These garments undoubtedly originated in those tropical climates where it is a necessity to cover every part of the body before retiring to rest, owing to the large number of insects which abound, and whose bite or sting is very irritating. In India, we are informed, the mosquito is a very troublesome pest in this way, and we have had customers who, having spent several years of their life in those parts, declare they would on no account retire to rest without their Pyjamas. In those countries they are generally made with feet, diagrams for producing which will be found in the Federation Prize Essay. The cheaper way of procuring Pyjamas is, of course, to get them ready-made. Most, if not all, of the respectable wholesale hosiers supply them at prices ranging from about 6s. 6d. the suit upwards. However, there are many occasions when it is necessary to make to order, and thus our reason for giving details of cutting, &c.

Jockey Suit. Figure 40.

The details of this will be easily gathered from figure, the jacket is cut as a small pyjama, and the breeches as coachmen's.

Spats, or Short Gaiters.
Diagram 79.

These articles are much patronized by young gentlemen, and although some consider they have a rather foppish appearance, yet they are very comfortable, keeping the feet very warm. If the quantities marked in the diagram are used by the inch tape a normal size will be produced, and if desired larger or smaller, use a graduated tape to reduce or enlarge them. They are generally made from drab Devon, the edges double stitched, and the seams stitched on either side, five or six buttons at the side, or they may be brought forward to follow the shape of front. It will readily be understood they consist of three pieces, one the full-size of diagram, another as outlined by 3, 6½, 6½, 9, 3, and another by 3, 0, ⅝, 7, ½, 3, with a button stand of from ¾ of an inch added. The simplest way of varying the size is to add to or take away from the back ½ an inch, as that will make a great deal of difference, quite as much as will be needed in ordinary practice.

Juvenile Clothing

We now come to deal with those garments which apply more particularly to those younger portions of the race which may be strictly called juveniles as compared with those a few years older, and whom we have designated youths, and to whom our former pages have been particularly devoted. Almost as much scope is allowed for the designer's skill in juveniles as in ladies clothing, inasmuch as neither colour nor material is restricted, so that with such scope the tailor must be very much to blame if he lacks the skill to produce a garment at once becoming stylish and attractive. Historical, national and artistic styles are all considerably patronized, and it occurs to us that this is one reason this branch of our trade has drifted into the hands of a few specialists, who make it their business to design or reproduce according to the style desired. It may be as well if we describe what we mean by historical, &c. Historical costumes refer to those worn in olden times, and which have become popular from a historical point of view. By national, we refer to the special costumes as worn by certain nations, such as the Scotch Highland Costume. By sectional, we refer to those garments worn by a certain part of the community by virtue of their trade or calling, and amongst which may be quoted: the Sailor and Military styles. By artistic we refer to such garments as are trimmed either by pleats (as in the Norfolk) or in braided designs, as illustrated on Plate 18. It will be noticed that in the following diagrams the back length has been reduced ¼ inch, and the front shoulder increased a like amount, thus altering the balance to the extent of ½ an inch, that being in accordance with the dictates of our experience; most juveniles resembling to a very large extent the corpulent figure, and being of the erect type demand this alteration in the balance of the garment. It is hardly necessary for us to repeat the arguments we previously used in favour of cultivating a juvenile trade, as they were dealt with in the early part of the present work, so that we will at once proceed to deal with the various costumes individually, and begin by one of the most popular National Costumes.

The Scotch Highland Costume.
Dias. 80 to 93. Fig 41. Plates 16 and 17.

A good deal of variation is permissible in some of the details as well as the material from which this is made, and as military garments form a kind of standard pattern which are worked out in these various points by authorized military regulations, we feel we could not do better than quote the Army Regulations for the Doublet of Highland Regiments.

"DOUBLET — Scarlet cloth, with collar and cuffs of the regimental facings. The. collar laced and braided according to rank,

Gauntlet cuffs, 4 inches deep in front and 6 inches at the back, edged with ½ inch lace round the top and down the back seam: 3 loops of gold braid with buttons on each cuff. 8 buttons in front, and 2 at the waist behind. Inverness skirts, 6½ inches deep, with skirt flaps 6 inches deep ; 3 loops of gold braid with buttons on each skirt flap. The front, collar, skirts and flaps, edged with white cloth, ¼ inch wide, and the skirts and flaps lined with white. Shoulder straps of twisted round gold cord, universal pattern, lined with scarlet; a small button of regimental pattern at the top. Badges of rank in silver".

The style in which the Highland Dress is made for little boys is as follows: it consists of the Doublet with tashes, (*i.e.*, small skirts), vest with flaps, kilt of Tartan of clan pattern, the Sporran or Pouch, the Plaid, the Claymore or Sword, the Dirk, the Skean Dhu, Brooches for cap and shoulder belt, the hose which should be of the same pattern as the Plaid or Kilt, but with the check running on the bias. The cap with one, two, or three feathers, according to the social position of the wearer, and fancy brogues with buckles, completes the costume. Illustrations of all these details will be found on Plate 17, and should our readers have any difficulty in procuring them, we shall be pleased to do so for them. The Claymore is worn on the left side, the dirk on the right, and the Skean Dhu in the stocking, whilst the position of the Cap and shoulder Brooches, as well as the Sporran will be thoroughly understood without any explanation of ours. Turning our attention to the diagrams for reproducing same, we find they are produced by the same system as previously explained, the various quantities marked on them being the usual shape given to the seams of this garment. The back is cut on the crease, and a button stand is left all down the front.

This, however, is not always done, many being made to just fasten at the neck, and have two rows of buttons, *i.e.*, one down each forepart. It is made to come just below the natural waist, and is continued below that with the tashes or skirts, which really form one of its principal features.

The Front Skirt,
Diagram 84,

Is not brought to the end of forepart being left open to show the vest between; its shape is faithfully portrayed in the diagram, and if the quantities there marked are used as units of the graduated tape, they will be reproduced of a suitable size. The underskirt is cut round, and has the edge finished in the same way as the edge of the Doublet, which our diagram illustrates as being round. The top tash, as will be seen, is pointed, and has three buttons and cords. These buttons are generally plate, diamond shape, and not unusually of silk or mohair, according to the material used. The diamond-shaped button, however, gives it a more decided Scotch tone, they having a thistle on them. The side tash is somewhat different in shape, the details of which may be readily gathered from the diagram. The back tash is decidedly different, and as shown on our diagram, shows the skirts for the whole back, that is, right and left; they are cut separately, and allowed to slightly overlap and left plain, no buttons or cords being put on them. 13 or 14 buttons are put up the front, and a shoulder strap either of cord or braid, or from the same material as the Doublet is placed on the shoulder, as in diagram 80. The sleeve is produced on precisely the same lines as previously described, the special feature of this being the gauntlet cuff, the size of which is clearly marked on diagram 81; it is left loose on the top edge, and lined with silk or the same as used for the body. The edges are finished

the same as the edges of Doublet and three buttons, and cords complete it as shown.

The Vest.
Diagram 75.

The special points about this are fastening to neck and cut long in front, with the corners cut sharply away, as illustrated. Flaps to the pockets of the shape shown, which are finished *all round* the same as the edges, the pockets being more usually put in above than under them. 3 buttons and cords are put on the same way as on the tashes. The back is cut much shorter than forepart, and a slit left at the side as shown, the reason for this is to prevent the possibility of the back showing if the back or side tashes were accidently lifted. We now come to the most distinctive feature of this dress; viz.

The Kilt.
Diagrams 86 and 87.

Which, as will be seen, consists of three parts, viz., the left, or top apron, which is usually finished with rosettes, &c., as illustrated, and is made at top rather more than waist, and 1½ inches wider at bottom. The centre or kilted part, when finished, is equal to remaining two-thirds of the waist: the right, or under apron, is the same size as the left, and is of course left plain. The great thing to be avoided in these is their opening in front from want of size for the movements of the body. The measures usually taken for a Kilt are 1½ or 2 inches above the natural waist to the knee bone for length, and the size round the waist and seat, the latter measure being more important with men than boys, there being comparatively little difference between the seat and waist of a boy.

These Kilts are frequently worn by adults, and as instructions for making will

not in all probability be found in any work, we give the following, the principal points of which appeared in No. 348 of the *Tailor and Cutter.*

Making a Kilt.
Diagram 88. Plate 17.

For a full-grown person a Kilt requires about six times the waist measure, or from 7½ to 9 yards; the quantity, however, further varies according to the thickness of the material, the degree of fulness desired, and the pattern, and the distance the stripes composing it are apart. Still, speaking of an adult, the depth of a Kilt is the width of the material, and is worn higher or lower on the body, according to the height of the wearer, and the distance he wishes it to cover the lower limbs. Properly, when standing, it should be level with the lower part of the knee, so that in the act of walking it does not touch the hinder part of the leg. For boys and youths the depth must be varied according to height.

Although to the uninitiated the making of a Kilt appears complicated, it is in reality very simple. Supposing it to be made of Tartan, the clan stripe must appear in the centre of each plait, which is easily distinguished by its prominence; this necessity is the reason of the peculiarity in plaiting up a Kilt. Diagram 88 shows the section of the plaits — that is, that the lines represent the edge of the material.

The *'s show the front of the plaits, the O's the back of them. In ordinary plaiting both back and front would appear the same. each plait running to a sharp point, as those represented by the O's, but then as a particular stripe, within given and limited intervals, must be shown on the front, that portion of the plait containing it is turned back upon itself; at least, that is the result arrived at, although not exactly the method followed, which we will describe.

When on, a Kilt appears to consist of two portions, the plaited, which is behind and over the hips, and the plain, which is in front. This plain part is called the apron, and is really double, each end of the Kilt having a quantity left plain, from ten to twelve inches, and in wear they are doubled over and under — the right under the left over. The number of plaits in a Kilt will vary with the size, but may be usually taken at about thirty, and in width must be regulated by size of waist; having fixed upon the width and number of plaits, keeping in view the quantity of material and the distance the stripes to be thrown up are apart, proceed to baste down each edge of the plaits from top to bottom, about five inches from the top, making them a little narrower, to hollow of waist. Having done this, carefully bring all the edges so basted together, one at a time, and baste firmly down from top to bottom, keeping the under material in the form of box plaits, that is, let it lie both ways, except the two front ones, which must all lie one way, backwards: having proceeded thus far, draw the edges together for about ten inches down, after which, firmly prick across the bottom of the sewed part of the plaits, through all. Turning now to the inside, the edges of the plaits may be felled or stitched down as far as the pricking across; or, what is far better (although not strictly regular), as it makes the Kilt thinner and set better over the hips, is to cut out all the material to the outside plaits, fill in the space with a piece of firm tweed, and line over it. In doing this shape to hollow of waist, for which purpose we have directed above that each sewed part of the plaits should be narrowed in the centre. By Saxons, Kilts are sometimes worn with braces, but the Celt draws his philabeg, firmly round his waist with pins five or six inches long, with silver or gold heads.

Bind the top; press the Kilt before removing the basting. This is not a very particular operation, but must be thoroughly and firmly done, so that every plait keeps its place, this and the forming of the waist being the two parts upon which its beauty depends. The next operation is to put on the straps and buckles, if worn, the straps of leather being put on the ends of the apron, opposite the hollow of waist, and the buckles in a corresponding line on the third plait; the under strap must of course pass through a hole to the top side. The last operation is to put on the rosettes, three on the edge of upper apron, and three down the edge of the corresponding plait, with strings of the same ribbon as the rosettes, passing from under them, so as to tie together.

To make a rosette, take a stiff piece of card cut round, and cover the same as a button with black cotton, then take a ribbon to match either the ground colour or that of the superior strip of the Tartan, about half an inch wide, draw in one edge and carry round and round from outside to centre, finishing with a small button covered with the same, or cut into about three inch lengths, and sew them on the double in rows, beginning with the outside and finishing as before, with a button in the centre.

Description of all the Clan Tartans.
Diagrams 91, 92 and 93.

With the view of making our description of the Highland Costume as complete as possible, we give these diagrams with descriptions of all the others which appear in the *Tailor and Cutter* for 1876.

NOTE. — The figures to the left of the diagrams of the clan tartans represent the number of EIGHTHS OF AN INCH, consequently there are 113 eighths in diagram 91, 69½ in diagram 92, 60½ in diagram 93. The clans chosen are solely for illustration.

At the top is the extent in eighths of an inch. Three threads are usually the quarter of an eighth, and at the bottom is the colour. A work illustrating the various tartans in the proper colours and proportions is published by Messers. W. & A. K. Johnston, price 2s. 6d.

All members of clans are naturally desirous of knowing their own tartan; and so frequent have been the intermarriages between the two countries, that numerous Englishmen feel interested in the same subject. A Highlander's clothing is his tribal insignia, and he literally displays on his shoulders his clan coat-armour. It may be useful to know one's clan and name by this means; and the following diagram and list will enlighten the enquirer into the science. It will also, it is hoped, serve to check a system of corruption to which of late years it has been so much exposed.

We shall now endeavour to make this matter clear, without having recourse to colours; and this, simple as it may appear, has never, we believe, been attempted. In tartans, the warp (or long thread) and the woof (or cross thread) are each of the same breadth, consequently the pattern is a square or chequer. It will, therefore, be necessary to give the length of the pattern only; that is to say, a series of colours complete; and these are repeated as often as required.

Buchanan.— ½ azure, 8 green, ½ black, 1 azure, ½ black, 2 yellow, ½ black, 1 azure, ½ black, 8 red, 1 white.

Cameron.— ½ yellow, 4 blue, 1½ red, 8 blue, ½ red, 8 black, 8 green, 1½ red, ½ green, ½ red, 4 green, ½ red, ½ green, 1½ red, 8 green, 8 black, ½ red, 8 blue, 1½ red, 4 blue, 1 yellow.

Campbell of Argyle.— 4 blue, 1 black, 1 blue, 1 black 1 blue, 8 black, 8 green, 1 black, 2 white, 1 black, 8 green, 8 black, 8 blue, 1 black, 1 blue, 1 black, 8 blue, 8 black, 8 green, 1 black, 2 yellow, 1 black, 8 green, 8 black, 1 blue, 1 black, 1 blue, 1 black, 4 blue.

Campbell of Braidalban.— 2 blue, 1 black, 1 blue, 1 black, 1 blue, 7 black, ½ yellow, 11 green, ½ yellow, 7 black, 6 blue, 1 black, 1 blue.

Chisholm.— 2½ red, 8 green, 2½ red, 2 blue, 1 white, 2 blue, 11 red, 2 blue, 1 white, 2 blue, 2½ red, 8 green, 2½ red, 1 blue.

Colquhoun.— ½ blue, 1 black, 6 blue, 9 black, 1½ white, 7 green, 1 red, 7 green, 1½ white, 9 black, 6 blue, 1 black, 1 blue.

Cumin.— 1 azure, 1 black, 2 azure, 5 black, ½ orange, 5 green, 2 red, ½ white, 2 red, 5 green, ½ orange, 5 black, 2 azure, 1 black, 2 azure.

Drummond.— ¼ white, 1 azure, 1½ blue, 4 red, 8 green, ½ yellow, 1½ blue, ½ white, 17 red, ½ white, 1½ blue, ½ yellow, 8 green, 4 red, 1½ blue, 1 azure, ½ white.

Farquharson.— ½ red, 2 blue, ½ black, ½ blue, ½ black, ½ blue, 4 black, 4 green, 1 yellow, 4 green, 4 black, 4 blue, ½ black, 1 red,

Ferguson.— ½ green, 6 blue, ½ red, 6 black, 6 green, 1 black, 6 green, 6 black, ½ red, 6 blue, 1 green.

Forbes.— 1 blue, 1 black, 6 blue, 6 black, 6 green, 1 black, 1 white, 1 black, 6 green, 6 black, 6 blue, 1 black, 1 blue.

Fraser.— 2½ blue, ½ red, ½ blue, ½ red, 5 green, 6½ red, 1 green, 6½ red, 1 green, 6½ red, 5 green, 5 blue, ½ red, ½ blue, ½ red, 5 blue, 5 green, 6½ red, 1 green, 6½ red, 5 green, ½ red, ½ blue, ½ red, 5 blue.

Gordon.— ½ blue, 1 black, 5½ blue, 6 black, 6 green, 1 yellow, 6 green, 6 black, 1 blue, 1 black, 1 blue, 1 black, 6 blue, 1 black, 1 blue, 1 black, 1 blue, 6 black, 6 green, 1 yellow, 6 green, 6 black, 5½ blue, 1 black, 1 blue.

Græme.— ½ black, 6 smalt, 6 black, ½ green, 1 azure, 8 green, 1 azure, ½ green, 6 black, 6 smalt, 1 black.

Grant.— (See Diagram 91.)

Gunn.— ½ green, 7 blue, ½ green, 7 black, 7 green, 1 red, 7 green, 7 black, ½ green, 7 blue, 1 green.

Lamont.— 2¼ blue, 1½ black, 1½ blue, 1½ black, 1½ blue, 6 black, 6 green, 1½ white, 6 green, 6 black, 6 blue, 1½ black, 1½ blue, 1½ black, 6 blue, 6 black, 6 green, 1½ white, 6 green, 6 black, 1½ blue, 1½ black, 1½ blue, 1½ black, 4½ blue.

Logan and Mac Lenan (a).— 1¼ red, 1¼ blue, ¾ red, ¾ blue, ¾ red, 7 blue, 5¼ black, 7 green, ½ red, ½ black, 1 yellow, ½ black, ½ red, 7 green, 5¼ black, 7 blue, ¾ red, ¾ blue, ¾ red, 1¼ blue, 2¼ red.

Mac Alaster.— 4 red, ½ light green, 3 dark green, 1 red, 1 azure, 1 red, ½ white, 1 red, 1 azure, 1 red, 3 dark green, ½ red, ½ white, 6 red, ½ azure, ½ red, 11 dark green, ½ red, ½ azure, 16 red, ½ azure, ½ red, 11 dark green, ½ red, ½azure, 5½ red, ½ white, ½ red, 4 blue, ½ red, ½ white, 2½ red, 3 dark green, ½ light green, 2 red, ½ light green, 3 dark green, ¾ red, ½ white, ¼ red, 2½/ blue.

Mac Auley.— ½ black, 9 red, 3½ green, 1½ red, 5 green, ½ white, 5 green, 1½ red, 3½ green, 9 red, 1 black.

Mac Donald (b).— 2½ green, ½ red, 1 green, 1½ red, 8 green, 8 black, ½ red, 8 blue, 1½ red, ¾ blue, ½ red, 5 blue, ½ red, ¾ blue, 1½ red, 8 blue, ½ red, 8 black, 8 green, ½ red, 5 green.

Mac Duff.— 4 red, 3 azure, 4 black, 6½ green, 3½ red, 1 black, 3½ red, 1 black, 3½ red, 6½ green, 4 black, 3 azure, 8 red.

Mac Dugal.— 3 red, 6 green, 1 red, ½ blue, 18 red, 2 crimson, 18 red, ½ blue, 1 red, 6 green, 6 red, 6 green, 13 crimson, 1 red, 3 crimson, 6 blue, 2 red, 1 green, 2 red, 18 green, 1 red, 1 crimson.

Mac Gillivray.— ½ blue, 2 red, ¼ azure, 2 red, 9 green, 1 red, 7 blue, ½ red, ½ azure, 18 red, ¼ blue, ¼ azure, 2 red, ¼ azure, ¼ blue, 18 red, ½ azure, ½ red, 7 blue, 1 red, 9 green, 2 red, ¼ azure, 2 red, 1 blue.

Mac Gregor.— (See Diagram 92.)

Mac Innes.— ½ black, 6 green, 1 red, ¼ black, 1½ red, ¼ black, 8 red, 1 yellow, 1½ red, 3 azure, 1½ red, ¼ black, 4 green, ¼ black, 1 red, 1 white, 1 red, ¼ black, 4 green, ¼ black, 1 red, 3 azure.

Mac Intosh.— 12 red, 6 blue, 2½ red, 10½ green, 4 red, ½ blue, 4 red. 10½ green, 2½ red, 6 blue, 24 red.

Mackay.— ¾ green, 7 corbeau, 1 green, 7 black, 7 green, ½ black, 7 green, 7 black, 1 green, 7 corbeau, 1½ green.

Mac Kenzie.— 3½ blue, 1½ black, 1½ blue, 1½ black, 1½ blue, 7 black, 7 green, 1½ black, 1½ white, 1½ black, 7 green, 7 black, 7 blue, 1½ black, 1½ red, 1½ black, 7 blue, 7 black, 7 green, 1½ black, 1½ white, 1½ black, 7 green, 7 black, 1½ blue, 1½ black, 1½ blue, 1½ black, 7 blue.

Mac Kinnon.— (See Diagram 93.)

Mac Lachlan.— 4 red, 1 black, 1 red, 1 black, 1 red, 8 black, 8 blue, 1½ green, 8 blue, 8 black, 8 red, 1 black, 1 red.

Mac Laurin.— 9¼ blue, 4 black, 1½ green, 1½ red, 3 green, ½ black, 1 yellow, ½ black, 3 green, 1½ red, 1½ green, 5 black, 18 blue, 5 black.

Mac Lean.— ½ black, 1½ red, 1 azure, 11 red, 5 green, 1 black, 1½ white, 1 black, ½ yellow, 2 black, 3½ azure, 2 black, ½ yellow, 1 black, 1½ white, 1 black, 5 green, 11 red, 1 azure, 1½ red, 1 black.

Mac Leod.— 1 yellow, ½ black, 6 blue, 6 black, 6 green, ½ black, 2 red, ½ black, 6 green, 6 black, 6 blue, ½ black, 2 yellow.

Mac Nab.— 1 green, 1 crimson, 6 green, 6 crimson, 6 red, 1 crimson, 6 red, 6 crimson, 1 green, 1 crimson, 1 green, 1 crimson, 6 green, 1 crimson, 1 green, 1 crimson, 1 green, 6 crimson, 6 red, 1 crimson, 6 red, 6 crimson, 6 green, 1 crimson.

Mac Nachtan.— ¼ black, ½ azure, 8 red, 8 green, 6 black, 4½ azure, 8 red, ½ azure, ½ black, ½ azure, 8 red, 4½ azure, 6 black, 8 green, 8 red, ½ azure, ½ black.

Mac Neil.— 1 white, 6 smalt, 6 black, 6 green, 2½

black, ½ yellow, 2½ black, 6 green, 6 black, 6 smalt, ½ white.

Mac Pharlan.— 10 red, ½ black, 5 green, 1 white, 1 red, ½ black, 1 red, 1 white, ½ green, 5 dark blue, 1 black, 1 red, 1½ white, ¾ green, 1½ white, 1 red, 1 black, 5 dark blue, ½ green, 1 white, 1 red, ½ black, 1 red, 1 white, 5 green, ½ black, 20 red.

Mac Pherson.— ¼ red, ½ black, ½ white, 5½ red, 2 azure, ½ black, ½ azure, ½ black, 2 azure, 3 black, ½ yellow, 4 green, 5½ red, 1 azure, 5½ red, 1 azure, 5½ red, 4 green, ½ yellow, 3 black, 2 azure, ½ black, ½ azure, ½ black, 2 azure, 5½ red, ½white, ½ black, ½ red.

Mac Quarie.— 2½ red, 12 blue, 15 red, ¼ azure, 2 red, ¼ azure, 15 red, 12 blue, 5 red, 16 green, 7 red.

Mac Rae.— 5½ green, 2½ black, 11 green, 2 red, 3 green, 1 black, 3 blue, 1 white, 3 blue, 1 black, 3 green, 2 red, 11 green, 2½ black, 11 green, 2½ black, 11 green.

Matheson.— ½ red, 1 green, 6 red, 5 dark blue, 1½ azure, 5 green, 1 red, 1 green, 1 red, 5 green, 6 red, 1 green, 1 red.

Menzies.— 14¼ red, 3½ white, 1½ red, 3½ white, 3 red, 1½ white, ¾ red, 7 white, ¾ red, 1½ white, 3½ red, 3½ white, 1½ red, 3½ white, 28½ red.

Munro.— 6½ red, ½ yellow, ½ blue, 1½ red, 13 green, 1½ red, ½ blue, ½ yellow, 1½ red, 3 blue, 1½ red, 1½ yellow, ½ blue, 13 red, 1½ green, 1½ red, 1½ green, 1½ red, 1½ green, 13 red.

Murray.— 1 blue, 1 black, 6 blue, 6 black, 6 green, 2 red, 6 green, 6 black, 1 blue, 1 black, 1 blue, 1 black, 6 blue, 1 black, 1 blue, 1 black, 1 blue, 6 black, 6 green, 2 red, 6 green, 6 black, 6 blue, 1 black, 2 blue.

Ogilvie.— 1 red, ¼ white, ½ black, ½ yellow, 1 purple, ½ yellow, 1½ green, ½ yellow, ½ red, ½ black, ½ red, ½ black, ½ red, ½ black, 1 yellow, 2 green, 1 yellow, ½ black, 2 red, ½ white, 2 red, ½ black, ½ yellow, 2 green, ½ white, 2 green, ½ yellow, ½ purple, 1 red, ½ black, 3½ red, ¼ white, ½ blue, ¼ white, 3½ red, ¼ white, ½ blue, 3½ red, ½ black, 1 red, ½ green, 1 yellow, 1½ green, ½ yellow, 1½ green, 1 yellow, 3 black, ¼ white, 1 blue, ¼ white, 3 black, 2 red, ½ white, 2 red, ½ white, ½ yellow, 3½ green, 1 black, 3½ green, ½ yellow, ½ black, 2 red, ½ white, 2 red, ½ white, 2 red, ½ black, ½ yellow, 2 green, ½ white, 2 green, ½ yellow, ½ black, 2 red, ½ white, 2 red, ½ black, 1 yellow, 3½ green, 1 black, 1¾ green.

Robertson.— ½ red, 1 green, 8½ red, 1 blue, 1 red, 8½ green, 1 red, 8½ green, 1 red, 1 green, 8½ red, 1 green, 1 red, 1 green, 8½ red, 1 green, 1 red, 8½ blue, 1 red, 8½ green, 1 red, 1 blue, 8½ red, 1 green, 1 red, 1 green, 8½ red, 1 blue, 1 red, 8½ green, ½ red.

Rose.— ½ red, 5 blue, 5 black, 5 green, ½ white, 2 black, ½ white, 5 green, 5 black, 5 blue, 1 red.

Ross.— 4½ green, 1 red, 9 green, 9 red, 1 green, 2 red, 1 green, 9 red, 9 blue, 1 red, 9 blue, 9 red, ½ blue, ½ red, 1 blue, ½ red, ½ blue, 9 red.

Sinclair.— 9 red, 10 green, 2½ black, ½ white, 4 azure, 18 red.

Skene or Clan Doucha' of Mar.— 1 black, 1½ red, 12 green, 2 black, 1½ orange, 2 black, 12 green, 2 black, 1½ red, 2 black, 12 blue, 2 black.

Stewart.— ¼ white, 1½ red, 1 black, 4 red, 8 green, 1 black, 1 white, 1 black, ½ yellow, 5 black, 3 azure, 16 red, 3 azure, 5 black, ½ yellow, 1 black, 1 white, 1 black, 8 green, 4 red, 1 black, 1½ red, 1 white.

Sutherland.— 5½ blue, 1 black, 1 blue, 1 black, 1 blue, 8 black, 8 green, 1 black, 8 green, 8 black, 8 blue, 1 black, 1 blue, 1 black, 8 blue, 8 black, 8 green, 1 black, 8 green, 8 black, 1 blue, 1 black, 1 blue, 1 black, 11 blue.

Urquhat.— 4 green, 1 black, 1 green, 1 black, 1 green, 8 black, 8 blue, 1 red, 8 blue, 8 black, 8 green, 1 black, 1 green.

(a) These two clans are of one descent, and there is no distinction in the tartans save that the latter prefer it of a broader pattern.

(b) There are four great divisions of Clan Donald, besides the chief branch distinguished as of "The Isles", viz., Clan Ranald, Glengarry, Keppach, and Glenco. The Glengarry tartan has a white stripe in the centre of the green division; and in that of Clan Ranald two have been introduced, one on each side of the same division.

(c) This is the original colour, from a native dye, but it is now usually dark blue.

The web of tartan is from 24 to 26 inches in width; and all clan tartans ought to have the colours so proportioned that they can be made up in the form of the kilt or the belted plaid; that is, the stripes should be so arranged, that in "box-plaiting" the distinguishing bars shall appear without any over-laying, which prevents the free play of the *Feilêbeag*, and destroys the pleasing effect of loose drapery. The ingenious fabrications of tartan which have for some time been so fashionable, are great improvements in this manufacture; and the brilliancy of colour and taste of arrangement are often extremely beautiful; but except where they are copies of clan tartans, they are arranged without any regard to their adaptation for the Highland dress. As they are, however, generally intended for fancy scarves and shawls, there would be less harm in this, were it not that patterns are often marked and disposed of as clan plaids to those who cannot tell whether they are so or not. Indeed the popularity of this national manufacture has induced parties to bring forward patterns as appertaining to clans and families, which are the entire emanations of their own inventive propensities; and although many are imposed upon by the plausibility with which the deception is supported, those who are at all versed in the subject can easily detect the true from the spurious.

By the plan here given, which is formed on that which appeared some 25 years ago in Mr. Logan's elaborate work on the Highlanders, any one will be enabled to provide himself with his appropriate Breacan. In many cases the scale here given will not, however, coincide with the pattern, as it may be of a larger or smaller *sett*; but, if correctly designed, the colours will proportionately correspond. Let the scale be drawn and the colours marked as far as given, which comprehends the whole pattern, and by applying it to a piece of cloth, the commencement being from the selvage, it will be proved correct or otherwise.

[Mr. Logan about the same time sent by letter the following information respecting Badges to *The Family Herald*.]

SUAICHEANTAIS* OR CLAN BADGES.

Buchanan (Dearc Fhraich), bilberry.

Cameron (Dearc Fhithioh) crowberry.

Campbell (Garbhag an t-sleibhe), club-moss.

Chisholm (Rainneach), fern.

Colquhoun (Braoileag nan con), bearberry.

Cumin (Dus mhic Chuimein), wild cumin.

Drummond (Lus mbic righ Bhreatninn), mother of thyme.

Ferguson (Ros Greine), little sunflower.

Forbes (Bealaidh), broom.

Fraser (Iughar), yew-tree.

Gordon (Eighearn), ivy.

Graeme (Buaidh craobh), native laurel.

Gunn (Aiteann), juniper.

Lamont (Luibhean), dryas.

Logan and Mac Lennan (Conas), furze.

Mac Aulay (Muileag), cranberry.

Mac Donald and all branches, as Mac Alasdair, Mac Intire, &c. (Fraoch gorm), common heath.

Mac Dugal (Fraoch dearg), bell-heath.

Mac Gregor and all branches of Clan Alpin, viz.; Mac Kinnon, MacQuarie Mac Nab, and Grant (Giuthas), pine-tree.

Mac Intosh, and all Clan Chattan — Mac Bain. Mac Gillivray, Mac Queen, Shaw, Farquharson, Davidson, Mac Duff, Mac Pherson, (Lus nam Braoileag) red whortle.

Mac Innes (Aonias), holly.

Mac Kenvie (Cuilfhionn), holly.

Mac Lean (Cuilfhionn), holly.

Mac Lachlan (Faochag), little perriwinkle.

Mac Laurin (Buaich craobh).

Mac Leod (Aiteann), juniper

Mac Nachtan (Lusan Albanach), trailing azalia.

McNeil (Luibhean), dryas.

Menzies (Fraoch nam Meinnich), Menzie's heath.)

Munro (Garbhag an Ghleann), commo n club moss.

Murray and Sutherland (Balaidh Chatti), butcher's broom.

Ogilvie (Boglus), evergreen alkanet.

Robertson (Dluith Fraoch), fine-leaved heath.

Rose (Ros mairi fiadhaich), wild rosemary.

Ross (Aiteann), juniper.

Urquhart (Lus leth'n t-Samhradh), native wallflower.

A chief carries three eagle's feathers: a duine-vasal, or gentleman, two: and a commoner, one only.

* Literally, the sprig of victory, a poetical term, because the laurel circlet was placed on the brows of those who had achieved triumph. Labhrail is the Gaelic name, whence the English laurel.

The various details illustrated in Plate 17 will be a very great help to tailors not acquainted with such. Diagrams 89 and 90 we shall refer to later on in dealing with Kilt Frocks in Sailor Dresses, etc., as they apply more particularly to them, although they are often used for a species of Scotch dress known under the name of the Highlands Undress Suit, an ordinary round jacket and vest, being worn with a kilt without any of the *et ceteras* which invariably go with the Highland suit proper, so that if our readers desire to make such they will easily be able to gain the necessary information from one part or another of this work.

This being the only style of national costume which is at all popular with juvenile wear we will leave out others of the same class and proceed to deal with

Artistic, Sectional, and Historical Types of Juvenile Costume.

It is somewhat difficult to subdivide these, as the Artistic runs parallel to the Sectional

and Historical on many occasions, so that we have

Military and Artistic Designs for Little Boys' Jackets.
Diagrams 94 to 105. Plate 18 Figs. 42 to 47.

Dealing first with the cutting of these it will only be necessary to point out the special features to be observed, as it is in all other respects produced by the same system as previously described. All that we noted in the remarks on Juveniles apply to these, and as they are generally made to fasten up to the throat it will be necessary to take the size of the neck into consideration, and with that end in view and to facilitate the matter we only make the front length from ⅝ to ¾ longer than the front shoulder, making up the size of neck at front, adding on the button-stand in the usual way, with the exception of Diagrams 100, 103, and 106, which are all made to fasten with hooks and eyes, and loops of braid or cord over buttons or olivets.

It will be noticed there are two distinct styles of braiding, independent of the cuffs, viz., vertical and horizontal, the former with the design or patterns of braiding running up and down the figure, and in the latter across, the effect of these on different types of Juveniles will be very striking, and the tailor may show a knowledge of artistic effect by the selection he makes for different forms. Diagrams 94, 96, and 97 are especially suitable for the podgy, fat boy, and Diagrams 100, 103, and 106 would improve the boy whose tendency is to the tall and thin type. Why this is so we will endeavour to explain. It is a well-known fact that stripes add to the size of the figure (apparently), in whatever direction they run, and as these designs of braiding have a very similar effect by producing a line in the direction the braid is put on. In Diagrams 94, 96, and 97 the most prominent line of

trimming running vertically cuts the figure, as it were, into sections and so reduces the width and increases the height, whilst those shown on Diagrams 100, 103, 106, running in the reverse direction add to the width and contract the height. Of course we are now speaking of the effect produced to eye, as we are apt to look at everything by comparison, and if this has not been demonstrated to our readers let them take 36 inches of material measuring say 40 inches (sideseam), and another 36 inches measuring only 24, and, forgetting the knowledge they both measure 36 inches long, look at them and see which appears the longer. They will soon see the effect of the narrower width. In just the same way stripes make the material appear narrow and long, and for this reason stripes are especially suitable for short, stout people, and large and prominent checks for tall and thin people. Light colours or those which attract the light has the effect of apparently increasing the size, whilst dark colours diminish it. To test this, put a light check coat on a stout man, and then get him to remove it and put a black one on him, and the apparent difference will be surprising. This is where art comes in in Tailoring, and the sooner tailors make themselves acquainted with a few of its general rules, or, if we may use a paradoxical term, the Science of Art, the sooner will the glaring errors that are daily walking about our streets be avoided.

Ladies have long since acknowledged this fact and put it into practice, hence the beautiful and graceful effect produced in many of their costumes. They certainly adorn the works of God, and the responsibility of taking lessons from them and applying the same to our everyday duties, so that our sex may appear the very embodiment of masculine strength and energy, devolves upon us. Let us awake to a sense of our duty and study our calling, practi-

cally, scientifically, and artistically, for it is impossible to attain the highest degree of excellence till we combine the teachings of these phases. We all know that one garment suits us and that another does not, but how few of us can deduce the rules which points us to the course of this effect, much less put them into practice, and advise our customers in their choice of style and material. It is a knowledge of such that makes the tailor an artist, and enables him to embody a grace of outline to the seams, to cut the shape of a suitable style, which, combined with a corresponding material, enables him to clothe his customers in a garment which shall hide all the defects of his figure, and bring into prominence every point of beauty. There is in this a study which will make his soul swell with a pride in his calling, and acknowledge that it is indeed noble, a science to be proud of, an art to develop, and, combining the whole, produce those coverings for his fellow creatures which makes them appear adorned and beautified images of our Creator. We trust our readers will pardon this digression from our subject proper, but art is a phrase of our calling so seldom developed, if not wholly ignored, that we could not let the opportunity slip without a few words, and we trust we shall not appeal in vain, for we are desirous of impressing on the coming as well as the present race of cutters the necessity of individual effort to maintain what the past and present race have achieved in placing their nation first in our particular calling amongst the civilized world. This can only be done by individual effort, and such will command individual recompense, for as we sow, so shall we reap, and if we make our profession a study in all its branches, we shall, in a few years, reap a commensurate golden harvest.

The Prince.
Diagrams 94 and 95. Figure 42.

This suit is made from diagonal, and trimmed with a bracket of wide fancy braid, traced all round with a Russia braid, in a fancy design which is both simple and effective. The pocket is put in slightly on the bias and traced round with eyes of Russia braid and finished off with crow's toes at the ends. The cuff, as illustrated on Diagram 95, is to match, whilst a similar design is placed on the side of the knickers. As will be seen, it fastens down the front with holes and buttons and an Eton collar finishes it at neck.

The Count.
Diagrams 96 and 98. Figure 43.

Illustrates the cuff and forepart of a similar design, though quite different in actual detail. As with the former, two widths of braid are used, the broad one of a fancy plaited design being placed at the back, and the front rows of Russia braid being laid on in fancy figures. The cuff is designed in harmony, and as with the former the knickers should be trimmed to correspond. Some very stylish effects may be produced by contrasting colours of braid such as a brown on a drab, and so on, but on this point it will be best for our readers to experiment, and then if they have a good eye for effect they will soon be able to decide what will produce the best style under the circumstances.

The Duke.
Diagrams 97 to 99. Figure 44.

This is another similar combination of broad fancy braid and a Russia. The effect of this design is very pretty, besides which it is very simple. Some of our readers may possibly experience difficulty in doing this braiding, and it might be of great service to them to know the name and address of a firm who do all kinds of braiding for the trade. Messrs. Lyons of 66 and 67, Milton Street, London, make this business a speciality, and do a large trade in it both for the wholesale and retail trades. There is still another plan which will help the tailor over the difficulty, viz., to use Mr. Briggs' transfer papers, which are arranged with the design on a piece of thin tissue paper, laid on the part desired to be braided, and a warm iron passed over it; this transfers the pattern to the cloth, when the braid can be easily run on the marks so obtained. Books of the various designs may be had from them at a very small cost, and the price of the papers is quite nominal. His address is 8A, Church Street, Manchester.

The Rifle.
Diagram 100. Figure 45.

This style is an adaptation of the style of trimming used for the Rifles of Her Majesty's army. The edges are corded and six drop loops are passed across the breast, the top one extending to the shoulder seams and gradually reducing in width to the bottom one. The double cord is formed in a loop top and bottom, and a netted button put on the top of the drop. Olivets are placed down the front on one side, and loops of the cord left on the other. The pocket is corded round with a crow's toe in centre of top, two loops placed at equal distances along the lower edge. The cuffs shown in Diagrams 101 and 105 are reduced from that excellent work, "Garment Making", published at the *Tailor and Cutter* Office, and show respectively the designs for braiding the cuffs of lieutenants, captain, and major of the Rifles. The more elaborate of these are hardly likely to be used for juveniles. Still, with a knowledge of

the correct thing, they may be utilized or modified to taste.

The Gordon.
Diagrams 102 and 103. Figure 46.

This is a very simple style of braiding, and is the same as on the statue of the late General Gordon in Trafalgar Square. It merely consists of braid laid on flat and the ends pointed and dropped over. This should properly be done with two rows of braid. It will, however, simplify matters if one wide one is used. As will be seen, this, too, is fastened down the front with hooks and eyes, and olivets put down the fronts, which makes a neat finish. A facing should be put all down the front to prevent the underclothing showing through between the hooks and eyes.

The Artilleur.
Diagram 106. Figure 47.

This is an adaptation of the Artillery Shell Jacket trimming where the cord is yellow on the blue cloth. It is very effective, and one which can be easily produced by any intelligent tailor. The edge is corded, as is also the pocket. The chief feature to notice is the finish at top and bottom. The front is finished with ball buttons, which are passed through the cord. This, however, is only done for ornament, it being fastened down with hooks and eyes as with the others. The cuff illustrated on Diagram 104 is the Regulation pattern for a Major of the Infantry, and is suitable for those on Diagram 100, or an adaptation may be used. There is another military design in Diagram 13, which shows the Infantry Patrol Jacket, and which is equally suitable for juveniles and youths, if not more so. These designs of braiding will give the principal ideas to be embodied in trimming juvenile clothing, and the further adaptation of it shown on

Plate 19 illustrates the application of braid, *i.e.*, to fancy materials, such as plush, &c. Plate 18, however, is the one which deals more particularly with braiding, and will be found quite sufficient illustration of this phase of artistic tailoring, especially if the points we have directed attention to are thoroughly understood.

Plate 19.

On this Plate is shown the application of silk, plush, velvet, and braid, and by which some very good effects are produced.

The Court.
Diagram 107. Figure 48.

This presents a modification of the old style of dress worn in the 17th century, when the gentlemen wore long coats, and their vests reached almost to the thighs. The Diagram is considerably modified, hence if that style of dress were required it would be necessary to make it longer. As represented here, the body of the coat and sleeves, as well as the breeches (diagram 113), are made of plush, and a false vest inserted down the front of silk. This latter may, of course, be made separately if so desired, and in which case diagram 114 may be followed; still, there are many suits made which have false vests inserted, which are all treated in this way, viz.: allowed to just go under the forepart, say at least a couple of inches, and then fastened to the lining; the pointed lace collar and cuffs invariably form a part of this costume. As regards the cutting of this suit, it is produced in just the same way as already described, the fronts of the jacket being cut away from the neck, to allow of the vest being seen, which buttons down the front. If it is made to come very low, it will be advisable to leave the bottom button about three or four inches below the waist, so that the bottom of the vest may not contract the action of the legs. Diagram 108 illustrates the cuff for this style of costume, and which is merely a plain cuff with a lace cuff put on afterwards.

Which is the right way to cut Velvets, &c.?

Is a question which often puzzles the tailor, as it seems so contrary to his ordinary practice to cut it with the pile running up, and he fancies he has heard that is the correct way. There is a difference of opinion on this point, and although it is generally considered correct with the pile running up, yet that plan is by no means universally adopted; for although it is generally conceded that when cut with the pile running up it presents a very much richer appearance, yet those who cut it with the pile running down contend that it wears very much cleaner, and does not catch the dust nearly as readily, and in brushing it the dirt can be more easily removed, so that our readers will see there is no universal custom, but in the absence of any instructions in this matter, he would certainly be safer in cutting all velvets, plushes, firs, &c., with the pile running up.

The Lancer.
Diagrams 110 and 111. Figure 49.

As will be gathered from these diagrams, the only variations in the cut are as follows: it is cut a trifle shorter and the forepart only cut to come to the breast line, the fastening of the front being affected by a kind of double lapel which allows of its being fastened over on either side, It certainly forms a very stylish garment, and is something out of the ordinary run, yet simple, and such that any tailor might make with ease. The style of trimming illustrated on the lapel, diagram 111, is both simple and effective, being formed by a crow's toe at either end, the buttonhole being in the centre of this, care should be taken to carefully conceal the ends of the braid, as if these are not out of sight, they detract very much from the finish of the garment, this style of suit blends itself very readily to what many firms call

The Four in Hand,

Owing to the ease to which it can be converted into various styles, for instance, the lapel might be braided one side and left plain or differently braided the other; then by leaving the lapels off, and fastening the fronts with hooks and eyes would make another style, whilst the fourth may be arranged by fastening the lapel inside and making it form a sham vest, as it were, the fronts left loose and open. At any rate there is plenty of scope for the display of ingenuity in dealing with juvenile clothing, still we do not think these fancy styles ever have a very large sale, people generally preferring to dress their children in plain useful garments; still, there are always a few who go in for novelties such as these, and those who make a leading line of this branch of the profession, should always have a few of this class to add character to their stock; if they make a display at all in their window, it gives a variety which is often very telling in obtaining customers.

The Regent.
Diagrams 109 and 112. Figure 50.

This is another very effective style of making up velvet, being flat braided with mohair braid on the edge, and trimmed up the fronts with a fancy braid. The fronts are arranged to fasten with hooks and eyes. some fancy buttons being put on the front edge to take off the plainness of this style of fastening. Diagram 109 illustrates the style of cuff to correspond. In giving this

illustration of trimming, we do not wish our readers to look on this in any other way than as a specimen of the style in which velvet and plush suits are made up by those houses who cater largely for the wants of juveniles, as, of course, the styles of trimming are innumerable, and it would be useless for us to attempt to describe them all, it being rather our aim to select a few of those which may be looked upon as representative styles, and of which plate 19 is composed. It also contains

The Court Breeches.
Diagram 113.

Of late there has been a very decided tendency to have the nether garments for boys to fit rather close at the knee; there can be no doubt they look very smart and stylish, and are particularly appropriate to wear with old styles of dress such as illustrated on Figure 48 and Diagram 107; they are usually finished with three buttons at the knee and sometimes a narrow band and buckle. The manner in which they are cut is very similar to that already described for trousers, still, it may be just as well if we go over the various points again, so that there may not be any difficulty in cutting these little garments. O to 14 is the side length to the knees and to 17½ the full side length, from 12 to 17½ is the leg length, now draw a line at right angles to 9 17½, from 12 to 12¼, from 12 to 6 is ⅓ seat to 9, ½ and on to 12¼, ⅔ and ¼ of an inch. Now draw a line up at right angles to 9, and another down from 6. Find the level of the natural waist by going up a fourth of the seat, and 1 inch, and then measure on this line ¼ waist, and ½ inch, and then draw the hollow of the fork, carefully avoiding making it too hollow. A very good rule is to make it about ¼ of an inch more than half the distance between 9 and 12¼. Now divide the width of the legs at knee and bottom equally on either side of line drawn at right angles to point 7, and if it is desired to have the buttons, to run forwards at the knee, the width of the topsides at the side seam may be reduced, and the extra width put on the undersides. The undersides are produced by the topsides; come up from 9 to 3, ⅛ and draw a line from 3 to 12, and by which draw the seat seam at right angles; make a pivot of the knee and sweep from O to 19, and then proceed to measure off the size of the seat and measuring from 9 to O, but on the natural waistline, and placing whatever quantity that is at 9 X, and measure towards 19 the waist plus the one inch consumed in the seams. Now measure the seat in the same way as the waist, but allowing from ½ to 2 inches for ease and seams. The mode of measuring the seat is as follows: Apply the tape to the forepart from S to E, then take the tape back to A on the undersides and make up the seat measure, and 1½ or 2 inches as just described. If these breeches are made to fit the knee very tight it will be as well to allow about ½ or ¾ inch to be fulled on over the knee of the topsides, but this is scarcely necessary unless they are made to fit the knee very close.

The Regent Knickers.
Diagram 115. Figure 50.

These are produced in precisely the same way as just described, the variation in the width of the legs being arranged equally on either side of the centre line. The dress should be taken out for all styles, although we know some people do not do this for little boys, still, if they wish them to fit smart and clean at the fork a small quantity must be taken out.

The Court Vest.
Diagram 114.

In order to illustrate the style of vest generally made to wear with suits of this class we added this diagram; it may either be reproduced by the graduated tape to agree with the breast measure, or by the divisions of the breast measure given on page 34. The only feature worthy of note is that it is made of the no-collar type and generally fastening close up to the throat. We also illustrate on this plate the principal style of collars worn by juveniles. For very little boys the lace pointed collar and cuffs are particularly appropriate and becoming, and for older boys there can be nothing better than either the plain or fancy style of Eton. We now come to deal with plate 20, which deals exclusively with

Varieties of Sailor Costume.
Diagrams 116 to 129. Figures 51 to 54.

Of all the styles adopted for juvenile wear there are probably none in such universal favour as the sailor suit, and which is worn by boys and youths of all ages with only some little variation in the details, thus, when the little one is first put into suits he generally has the sailor blouse and a kilt, then he comes to wear knickers, and then very soon the regular jack-tar trousers, and as this style is so universal, we have little doubt this plate will prove one of unusual interest, and in anticipation of this we shall treat of it as fully as possible. We begin with

The Sailor Blouse.
Diagram 115. Figure 51.

This is produced on the same lines as previously described for the shirt, but as this diagram is arranged somewhat differently, it will be as well if we describe it again. Square lines O 18, O 20. From O to 2½ is ⅙ neck, from O to ¾ is always ¾ of an inch, from O to 2½ is ¼ of an inch more than an eighth; from O to 9 is half the breast and continue on to 17, the full length the garment is desired, plus whatever amount it is desired to "bag over" at the waist, whilst an inch of round is put on to compensate for hollowing tendency of the drawing in at the waist; now square across from all these points, and make 2½ to O, ½ breast, and continue on to 11¼ whatever amount of ease you may decide to give your blouse, in this instance we have made this 2¼ inches, or equal to ⅛ of the breast. 13½ is the same distance from 11¼ as 11¼ is from 9, and from 13½ to 22½ is a fourth of the breast, point 20 is ⅙ of the neck back from this, and draw the shoulder slope from 20 to 13½ of the front, and 2½ to O of the back, and then draught the scye by hollowing the front 1 inch in front of line 13½. The front may be advanced slightly at the waist; and a button stand added all down the front if it is desired to fasten it in that way, the same amount of round is added on the front at the bottom as at the back; as described, this will produce a moderately loose-fitting blouse, but if it is desired to fit looser the extra width which would be placed mostly at the waist would be equally distributed at the back under the arm, and on the front, putting twice as much under the arm as at either back or front; for instance, if it were desired to add 2 inches at the waist it would be distributed in this manner; 1 inch would be put in at the side, ½ an inch added to both the back and front; these garments are generally made up with a whole back, and put into a band at the waist, or a hem put all round the bottom and a piece of elastic run through it. A patch pocket is generally added, trimmed in the same style as the collar.

The Sailor Collar.
Diagram 119.

This readily explains itself as it shows how these are produced. As will be seen, it is the same as is used by the majority of the trade to produce the Three-quarters Circle Cape; and merely consists in putting the back and forepart together at the shoulder and making the centre of the collar to run with the back seam; whilst the size is entirely a matter of taste although the diagram illustrates a very suitable one, and which is made nearly as wide as the back and to come nearly to a level with the bottom of the scye. It is shown on this diagram as rolling rather low, but if desired it can be made to fasten close up to the throat, but in that case it loses much of its grace. It is generally trimmed with three rows of narrow white tape or braid, the rows being kept ⅛ of an inch apart. An anchor is generally, or at least often, put in the corner as shown, but this is not in accordance with those worn by the genuine sailor. A silk handkerchief is put round the neck and fastened just below the collar with a sailor's knot, whilst the buttons generally used are gilt anchor.

The Material

From which these are mostly made is ordinary blue Serge and trimmed with white tape, which is the same as used by sailors generally. Some very pretty effects are often produced by arranging contrasting shades of cloth or velvet in this style whilst a very large number are made for summer wear from white drill with blue Jean collars and cuffs; the various patterns of Galatea are also extensively used for this type of garment. We now come to

The Sleeve,
Diagram 118.

This is very simple. Draw line O 25, and make from O to 2¼ the same as 9 to 11¼ of the forepart, whilst, if it is desirable to put the sleeve in quite plain, 2¼ to 10 may be made the same as half the scye, and if pleats are desired, as is often the case, the extra width must of course be allowed for them between 2¼ and 10. The length of the sleeve is made to measure, and the width of the cuff fixed to taste, pleats being arranged here also; the bottom of the sleeve is generally finished with a cuff as is illustrated on Diagram 123. As will be readily gathered, the sleeve is cut on the crease, the seam coming under the arm and going into the scye at 11¼ on the level of scye line; this Diagram also shows the position of the good conduct stripes and the marks of distinction. These are worked in gold for the full dress; in red worsted on the blue serge, and in blue worsted on the white drill ones. This style of jacket may either be worn with the knickers as illustrated by Diagram 115, but of course cut from material to match the blouse, or with

The Ordinary Kilt Frock.
Diagram 126. Figures 52 and 52a.

We have already gone into the question of Kilt Frocks somewhat fully in dealing with the Highland Costume, so that it will be quite unnecessary to make more than a few passing comments.

This Frock forms, as it were, the connecting link between the little boy-baby and the little man just breeched, and, although more generally worn in connection with the Sailor Blouse, it allows of some of his undergarments being retained; yet it is quite suitable to wear with many other styles of jacket such as are to be found in this volume, then, again, it is suitable for girl's wear, as in figure 52A. There can scarcely be said to be any cutting required although there should be a certain amount of spring over the seat to allow of sufficient freedom for the legs, so that before the kilts are definitely fixed, it should be seen that they agree with the Diagram. O to 18 is the half waist, and from which square down 9 and go out 1½ inches on either side, and hollow the top at the waist ¾ of an inch. These are sometimes made up on a

foundation, in which case it would be cut in this way: the manner of arranging the kilt is shown on Diagram 89, whilst diagram 90 shows the method of arranging the box pleat. It should always be the aim of the cutter to preserve harmony throughout the Costume, so that if the Jacket is trimmed it will be advisable to trim the skirt in the same manner.

The Genuine Jack Tar Frock & Trousers.
Diagram 119 to 125. Figure 53.

These are taken from our work on Naval Uniforms which recently appeared in the monthly parts of the TAILOR AND CUTTER. Diagrams are marked out to the 36 size, so that all our readers will have to do will be to select a graduated tape to agree with the breast measure they wish to reproduce, and mark off the same quantities as are here marked with it, or they may be reproduced as follows: make the width ¾ entire breast A, midway, the armhole at 10 1 inch more than ¼ breast, and the sides hollowed 1 inch, A to 3 ⅙ neck. The sleeve head, as at 13, is cut 2 to 3 inches larger than the armhole, which is pleated in at top, as also is the bottom to the cuff.

As this is a duly recognized part of Naval Uniforms, it will be as well if we give the Admiralty Regulations respecting them, which run as follows: "Trousers of navy blue cloth or white duck, fitting tight at the waistband, to be tied at the back with black silk ribbon or white tape, with a pocket and broad flaps, and stained bone or white metal dead-eye buttons."

"White Frock to be made of drill, with collar and wristbands of blue jean, the collar having a border of three rows of three-sixteenths of an inch, white tape one-eighth of an inch apart, and the wristbands to be peaked with two rows of white tape along the upper margin and one along the lower, with one metal dead eye button at

the wrist. The blue Frock is just the same, except the collars and cuffs which are of the same material."

"Collars. — All seaman's collars are to be of the dimensions given on diagram 119."

Designing.
Diagrams 130 to 137. Figures 55, 56, 57, 58 & 59.

Probably there is no branch of the trade that requires as much skill as designing in order to produce successful results, and it is one that is probably less cultivated than any other. We are content to jog along in the same style year after year, when probably all around us are striving their utmost to introduce improvements or changes which will increase their trade; and as it is clearly our interest to produce changes in the fashion as speedily as possible, it must be apparent to all that the designer's art plays a very important part in the moulding of our fortunes. During Mr. D.E. Ryan's visit to England he laid very great stress on this point, and the method of designing we now explain is the same as he advocated and practiced, and as he is probably one of, ifnot the most successful designers we know of, we may justly look upon his method as a good one. His plan, then, was to have a piece of cloth and mark the pattern of a boy's jacket, such as is illustrated on Diagram 130, and have the same stitched in coloured silk on the cloth, so that whenever he wished to design a new style he would take this piece of cloth which he called "the designer", and set to work to either alter the position of the seams, insert a pleat or a series of pleats, put a yoke on the shoulder, and so on, till an altogether new style of dress was the result, his designs were looked upon as the best in the United States; so that our readers may safely take a hint from such an authority; for, although, to use a tailor's phrase, it is only "striking brights", yet that is just where the originality comes from, and

which we are apt to so often deplore as being lacking in our trade. It is not necessary we should describe the few examples of designing we give in minute detail, as our readers will be able to easily follow how these are produced, as the dotted marks show Diagram 130 in each case. When pleats are added they are generally laid on, and when they are inserted as in

The Yoke Norfolk,
Diagram 131, Figure 55,

The forepart is cut down and a piece inserted large enough to form the pleats, the seam being carefully hidden under the folds of the material. This style or design might be produced with straps laid on and stitched through the front and terminating at the pocket-mouth.

The New York.
Figure 56. Diagram 132.

This design, or one very similar to it, emanated from Mr. Ryan, and was considered a very pretty and stylish dress. It consists of the foreparts and back being cut away and pleats put up front and back to go under this deep yoke as it were. It is very suitable for little boys' wear.

The Brighton.
Figure 57. Diagram 133.

In this the same idea is developed, but in addition to the piece inserted in the front to form the pleats a sham vest is inserted, and showing 2 buttons below the coat; this may of course be a real vest if so desired; but they look very well just put to the front of jacket as illustrated.

The Dresden.
Diagram 138.

This is a really pretty style of dress, and consists of a loose-fitting body part made D.B., and put into a band at waist, below which small skirts are put on as with the

Doublet, only smaller and consequently more in number.

The Monte Carlo.
Diagram 139 Figure 59.

This is a very dressy suit for little boys, and is, as will be seen, an adaptation of the Gents' Dress Lounge. It makes a very pretty suit for little boys' evening wear at parties, especially if a light vest is worn as on figure 59. The lapels of coat should be faced with silk.

The Négligé.
Diagram 140

This is an adaptation of the Sailor Dress. It is loose-fitting and drawn into a band at the waist, buttons to the throat, and has a pointed Sailor collar. It was very much worn a few years ago, but has given place to the more modern styles such as are illustrated on Plates 18, 19, 20, and 21.

The Sydenham.
Diagram 137. Figure 58.

This is very suitable for plush or velvet with silk facings or vest of a contrasting colour. The scope for variety this opens up is very wide, and consequently there should be no lack of variety in the juvenile department, and if a really smart man possessed of an artistic taste and in addition a fair amount of originality were to take this matter up we are convinced he would succeed. The jacket is cut much longer than the rest of the diagrams on this page, it representing the Historic or 17th Century Dress.

We will now proceed to deal with two or three styles of little boys' Overcoats, and foremost amongst these we find

The Scarborough.
Diagrams 141 and 142. Figure 60.

This is really an Inverness, but with the cape extending all round, and which have been very popular during the past season. They undoubtedly possess advantages over the old style, as whilst they fit the body much closer, they are yet very much freer in wear, there being an absence of that contraction so often experienced in the old style. The method of cutting them is the same as previously described for Overcoats, with the exception that the scye is made very much deeper, a little more or less is of no consequence, as they have no sleeves in them; there is nothing taken out between the back and forepart at the waist as it is not desired to make them too close-fitting in the waist. The diagram illustrates the back as slightly hollowed, but this is often made whole, and in which case the back seam would be from the back tacking to the top O; as will be noticed, there is plenty of spring allowed at the bottom, a very necessary point, especially for little boys who are wearing kilts, &c., and in which case the amount (3 inches of overlap) we have illustrated may be increased with advantage. A button stand is left down the front, 1½ inches wide, and it is made to button through almost to the bottom. The cape portion of this garment is cut as follows, (see diagram 142). Place the forepart down as illustrated, and mark round the forepart at gorge, shoulder and down the scye for a few inches, say 3, and then mark upwards again, so that about ½ an inch V will be taken out, let this part come about 1 inch above the shoulder, and then place the back with the shoulder point touching it, and the back seam running at right angles to the front, and mark round the back shoulder, neck, and backseam; then mark off the length you desire it in the back, and then measure down from the neck point of front shoulder this same quantity, plus ¾ of an inch. The side length may be obtained in a similar manner, but adding from 1½ to 2 inches; now, if you

desire to have a very close-fitting Cape, you may reduce the width round the bottom by taking out a V from the bottom of from 3 to 4 inches, (but using care the size is not reduced round the shoulders) as per dot and dash line. These garments are generally finished with a Prussian collar and patch pockets, whilst tabs are often put in to prevent the Cape flying up in the wind; these are placed one in the centre of the back and one on each forepart. We now come to

The Kilt Overcoat.
Diagram 143 & 144. Figure 61.

This is another illustration of over-garments for little boys' wear who have not yet got out of their petticoats. As will be seen it is very similar to the last with the exception that the scye is filled up and sleeves added. We have duly noted the characteristics of little boys, viz.: as large at the waist as at the chest, as well as being decidedly erect. This, it will be noticed, we have arranged for by taking ½ of an inch from the depth of scye on the back, and adding it to the front shoulder measures, whilst the over-shoulder remains the same. The sleeve is produced on the same lines as already described; we merely give the diagram here so that those who use graduated tapes might have the diagram complete. These are often made to fasten up to the throat without a collar, as lace and other fancy styles of collars are worn with them. All kinds of materials are used for this, and probably there are few which produce a prettier effect than plush; but of course, that is for very little children. We now come to

The Austrian.
Diagram 145. Plate 23. Figure 62.

This is more especially suitable for a little boy in his first suit, and is certainly one of the prettiest garments we have seen for boys at this age. It is generally made from a blue beaver trimmed with astracan and ornamented with five rows of tubular braid, finished at the ends with crows' toes. The braid is allowed to go beyond the fore-part in order that it might fasten to the barrel on the opposite side. It will be noticed it is cut rather short, and there is not nearly as much spring as in the last one, but with these exceptions it is cut on similar lines, although in this case the measures are only taken, over the vest, and in the last it would be taken over the dress on which it would be worn This brings us to nearly the last diagram illustrative of style, viz.: —

The Real Little Lord Fauntleroy.
Diagram 146. Figure 63.

This style has been forced into popularity by the play bearing a similar name; it is certainly unique and artistic, although slightly effeminate, the leading feature as will be gathered, is the sash, whilst the lace collar and cuffs are also very conspicuous. As will be noticed, the jacket is very short (although they are often cut longer than our illustration), and the breeches tight-fitting, see diagram 113 and figure 62; the sash, however, prevents its looking by any means bare as it goes over the bottom of the jacket, and the ends hang over the breeches. The material from which these are generally made is velvet, plush, and similar materials, but, of course, it is by no means confined to either, as anything that forms a good contrast would be equally suitable. As it is not necessary at this stage to show the system for producing with every draught, we have drawn this by the aid of the designer, and if it is required to reproduce it by graduated tapes the same quantities may be taken as are marked on Diagram 130. The last diagram relating to this branch is a reduced model of gaiters and which if reproduced by the ordinary inch tape, will be suitable for a boy or girl of about 8 years of age; the

measures are as follows: length 16, knee 10½ small 9¼, calf 10½ ankle 8, and bottom 15. These are a good deal used in some districts and are very useful in cold and dirty weather, we now give a chapter on

Variations and Alterations.

One of the things that often puzzles the cutter in daily practice is how to produce ease in the scye and as we recently had a student write to us in this difficulty we thought it would probably be of use to other of our fellow craftsmen, as it enabled our ex-student to avoid a kill. He had been trying the old dodge of sinking and advancing the scye, but as soon as the customer lifted his arms it was almost unbearable. Of course, the scye had been made very much too deep and when the arms were raised the whole garment rested on them. We sent him a diagram the same as this, told him to rip his sleeves out and collar off and bring the coat up to its proper position on the figure; then take his pattern and put either one or two wedges in the original pattern and have his coat finished in this altered form. We afterwards had the pleasure of hearing from him that the alteration was highly successful, and that now he was glad the alteration had occurred as it had taught him a valuable lesson, so our readers may take a timely hint, and if they know their customers are particularly tender at this part they may make this provision in their coat at the start, and although it may not fit quite as clean just in the front of the scye, yet that will be overlooked by the customer in the fact that he has got a comfortable coat at last. Of course, we do not give this as a cure-all, but we are pretty sure this will prove effectual in nine cases out of ten, the principal causes of tightness in the scye being insufficient distance from the centre of back to the front of scye; insufficient depth, and a too crooked cut shoulder, a too short front shoulder, or a too short collar, all of which have a very similar effect.

Straightness and Crookedness.
Diagram 149.

Such a difference of opinion exists on what really constitutes this or whether such a thing really exists, that we felt we ought to give just a few lines to its elucidation as far as lies in our power.

The popular idea of straightness and crookedness is a deviation in the location of the neck point either forwards or backwards the advanced neck point being called straight, and the receded one crooked; but inasmuch, as there are so many variations which alter it in this way it is hardly a satisfactory definition; for instance, if the collar-stand or part of it were cut in one with the forepart, that would not make the garment straight, nor would the cutting away of the shoulder, as in a lady's evening bodice, make it crooked, so that it is necessary to advance a step further and to define it more closely.

The Straight and Crooked Shoulder.

Straightness and crookedness of the shoulder is shown on Diagram 149. As will be seen, lines are drawn at the level of neck point 1, the level of shoulder point 2, and the level of bottom of scye 3, all parallel to each other. Taking the shaded pattern as the normal, the dot and dash line shows the straight shoulder, all the points being advanced on lines 1 and 2, say 1 inch, the lower part of the pattern remaining the same, whilst the reverse operation, viz.: shifting the points backwards, as in dotted lines, produces the crooked shoulder. But these are variations which lead to no practical results, and if done to any extent, are only of service to produce misfits and alterations, hence we are constrained to say that this is false straightness and crookedness, and is only a complication of disorders upsetting the balance, the shoulder slope, and the length of front-edge in such a way as will destroy the fit of any garment. The crooked shoulder shortens the distance from nape of neck to bottom of scye in front as covered by the front shoulder. It lengthens the distance from the shoulder point to front of scye, or that part covered by the over-shoulder measure. It also lengthens the front edge. If the front edge is drawn in sufficiently to make it fit snug to the figure in front the result will be creases on the front shoulder, as the neck-end of front shoulder has been shortened, and the scye end lengthened; this will at once be seen by referring to Diagram 149. It is a very erroneous notion to fancy that straightening the shoulder in this way produces ease in the scye, for it actually reduces its circumference. The best way to do that is as we have pointed out in Diagram 148, and is the same in result as if the front shoulder and over shoulder measures had been increased, the latter in greater ratio than the former, whilst ½ an inch will be plenty to add to the front shoulder when sweeping from front of breast; but people who adopt this method must not expect their garments to fit as clean and smart as when produced to the customers' measures. We have seldom found it necessary to resort to such an alteration as this, having always been able to give quite sufficient ease by giving a proper shape to the scye, and cutting it to the customer's measures. As we call the alterations shown on diagram 149 false, it will be necessary for us to show what in our judgment is

True Straightness and Crookedness.
Diagram 150.

This is nothing to do with the shoulders, the front edge being the only part affected, for although it apparently alters the location of the neck point to others, yet the shoulders in all the three shown in Diagram 150 are identical, the variations introduced being nothing more nor less than a wedge inserted or taken from the front edge, the former producing a rounder and so a crookeder *front edge*, and the latter a straighter one. Now let us examine the requirements of any figure there and what do we find but that every figure is hollow down the middle of front, and as the proper way to fit a hollow is by the shortest distance between two points, and as any one with the least knowledge of geometry knows that is found in the perfectly staight line. Now this is what is required in the front, and if the garment is to fit satisfactorily, the centre must either be cut straight or manipulated straight, drawing any round there may be in till the straight is produced, But a feature comes in which must be studied in successful cutting, viz.: providing a proper receptacle for the breasts in just the same way that we provide room for the blades. This is done in the system laid down in this volume by adding to the front shoulder measure 1 inch, which extra 1 inch of length should always be drawn in, and the fulness worked back over the breast, so that if we have a prominent breast to provide for as is often found in the erect, we should add 1½ and in the flat-chested or stooping, ½ inch only, always drawing in the forepart to the straight line, for no matter whether the figure be stooping, normal or erect, the straight front edge will fit him, provided there is a sufficient receptacle for the breast. To assert that a wedge inserted in the side of forepart at waist to nothing at bottom of scye is identical with cutting the forepart across and lengthening the front edge as shown by dot and dash lines, is one of the most ridiculous, short-sighted assertions that could possibly be made, for surely in the one case the forepart is made *wider* and in the other *longer,* the former would produce room over the sides, and has nothing whatever to do with straightness and crookedness, whilst the latter has all to do with it, and if properly manipulated would produce room for the breast, and add greatly to the form and style of the garment. We trust this will be clear to our readers, but as it is a subject that requires an elaborate treatment we are only able to touch on the principal features, and hope it will set our readers thinking, when we doubt not they will soon form a definite conclusion as to what is true and what is false. We leave this subject by briefly referring to Diagram 151, which was recently referred to in the TAILOR AND CUTTER under the title of

What is the Result?

When the following supposititious case was given: A coat was cut for a customer and an inlay left all down the front of 1 inch, the coat was tried on and was found to fit splendidly, the tailor had the coat given back to him with instructions to finish it as it was, but by some means the inlay down the front got put into the garment, and as may be readily imagined the coat was too large. The cutter in order to rectify this error had the coat taken in under the arms and the scye advanced. Now the result of this operation was to make the coat 1 inch more crooked in the shoulder, and consequently the coat was a misfit, and which will be readily seen would be quite different to the straightness and crookedness shown on Diagram 150. Having far exceeded the space we had allotted to the consideration of this question, we will hasten on to consider the

Alterations to make for Abnormalities- Erect and Stooping Forms. Dia. 152.

This diagram shows at a glance the variations we should make for these figures, and may be summed up as shortening the back and lengthening the front for an erect form, and a longer back and shorter front shoulder for a stooping form, unaccompanied with either a prominence or flatness of blades or breast, both very unusual, for the erect man is generally flat at the blades and prominent at breast, the stooping figure the reverse. If our readers will only train themselves to take the measures we have explained, with accuracy, they will bring the garment out to the right shape as far as the body is concerned by the ordinary workings of the system, merely ranging the quantities taken out between back and sidebody to provide for prominent or flat blades, and the amount added to front shoulder for prominent or flat breasts. We know the measures cannot always be taken, so we give those methods generally practised by the most successful cutters of the present day for our readers' use when working from the scale or divisions of the breast. Probably there is no method of alteration for stooping and erect figures so widely practised as that shown on Diagram 153, and which merely consists in a wedge being inserted in the back and a similar one taken out of the front for a stooping figure, and the wedge out of the back and put in the front for the erect figure; this method is thoroughly reliable, and we do not know of a better for three seamers or lounges, but in body coats we prefer a straighter backseam, taking out more between back and sidebody both top and bottom, which we are convinced is more correct in principle and practice.

High and Low Shoulders. — Long and Short Necks. Dia. 152.

This diagram illustrates our method of treating these variations of build when we are unable to take our own measures: it is not necessary we should say more than to note the alterations marked F are those to

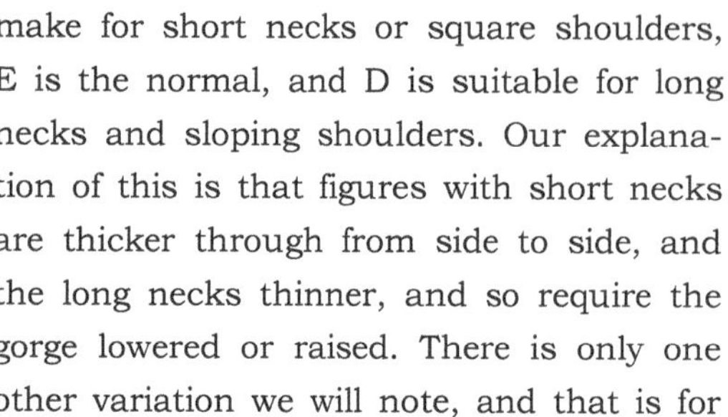

make for short necks or square shoulders, E is the normal, and D is suitable for long necks and sloping shoulders. Our explanation of this is that figures with short necks are thicker through from side to side, and the long necks thinner, and so require the gorge lowered or raised. There is only one other variation we will note, and that is for corpulent and slender waists, and as the principle is the same for both vests and coats, we have given the diagram on a vest, see Diagram 164.

The first thing to decide on is, what will be your standard of proportion. As the diagrams are drawn out in this book the waist is 4 inches smaller than the chest, so that whenever any variation exists it may be distributed $\frac{1}{3}$ at the side, and $\frac{2}{3}$ at the front, and the front lengthened at bottom $\frac{1}{3}$ and when an extreme case of corpulency occurs add on rather more at the front, and take out rather more at the side for a very thin one.

We will now briefly point out the remedy for a few of the leading misfits and then draw our labours to a close by a reference to the economy lays on the last Plates.

Creases in the Front Shoulder.
Diagram 155.

These may invariably be traced to a too crooked shoulder, which has produced a shortness from A to B and an excess of material at C, the result of which is, the creases down the front shoulder, which have puzzled so many, the remedy is to let out both forwards and upwards so as to increase the length from A to B, and if considered necessary take off a small quantity at C, and in most cases this will prove satisfactory. Of course, like most other defects, it may arise from other causes, and amongst these we mention a too short collar and canvas or facings twisted, whilst we have known a too hollow front shoulder to produce this.

Coat Winging away Behind.
Diagram 156.

This is a defect that is often seen in both lounges and morning coats, and as it is one that can easily be remedied, we thought a diagram showing how it might be rectified would be useful. It generally arises from a too long front shoulder, or what is practically the same thing a too short back, for, of course, the balance is governed by the relative lengths of the back and front shoulders, consequently the correct alteration is shown on Diagram 156, and which consists in ripping the shoulder through and then re-adjusting it when on the figure. This is the plan many cutters adopt in order to get the correct balance when trying on and is undoubtedly the most satisfactory plan next to direct measurements. This defect sometimes arises from the front edge not being properly worked up, when the remedy suggests itself. We now come to deal with what is probably one of the most frequent defects met with in lounge and similar garments, viz.:

Fullness at the Top of Sideseam,
Diagram 157

This too arises from various causes, amongst which we may mention a too short front shoulder, or what has the same effect, a too short collar; or the waist too much suppressed between M and L: or it is kept too flat at K, then again it often arises from a difficulty in landing the necessary fullness over the blades, and consequently the suppression at that part causes the fulness at the back of the scye, in each case the remedy suggests itself. Some advise the taking out of a wedge as from G to H, and which makes the back seam rather round as per dot and dash line at L and J, which clears the back of scye, but is apt to land surplus length in the centre of back; it is always advisable to let the sideseam take

the shape shown by the dot and dash line at K.

This, we think, will be sufficient to put the intelligent cutter on the right track, and that is all we desire to do in this work, which is not specially devoted to alterations. If our readers desire a more elaborate treatment, they could not do better than procure a copy of the "Art of Trying On", as that deals with this branch of our profession in a thoroughly exhaustive manner, still a hint is often sufficient to put the cutter on the right track. We have selected a few of the most frequent sources of trouble, and on which we have the most enquiries through the Editor's Table.

Tightness at the Top Button.
Diagram 158.

This generally arises from a too straight cut shoulder, in which case the remedy is, of course, to crooken it, as shown by the dotted lines at that part; but this is not always the cause as it often arises from an insufficiency of room in the sleeve head, this is especially the case when this defect is apparent in ladies' garments, and as of course it is necessary to treat every defect in accordance with its cause, so the remedy is to increase the width and round of the sleeve head. The next defect we will notice is in connection with vests, viz.,

Vests Rising in the Neck when Seated.
Diagram 159.

This is caused through a tightness on the shoulder point, and consequently the remedy is to let it out at that part, the alteration being clearly defined by the dot and dash line. The defect arising from the opposite cause to this is

Vest Standing away in Front.
Diagram 160.

This arises from a too short front edge or an insufficient length from the neck point to the bottom, and, as will be seen, the remedy is to lengthen it at the neck point as per dotted line.

Too Low at the Back of Neck.
Diagram 161.

This defect can be easily remedied by taking it in at the centre of back and letting it out at the side.

Creases Across the Front of Vest at the
Waist. Dia. 162.

This, although by no means a serious defect, yet is a very unsightly one. may arise from various causes, amongst which we may mention insufficiency spring at the hips, causing the vest to ride up at that part, or the customer has drawn the buckle and strap too tight. Or, it may be produced by a too long front edge, and of course the remedy in each case suggests itself. We will now give a

Plan for Lengthening Vest.
Diagram 163,

Which, although a very simple matter, yet is clearly one that is not universally understood, as was evidenced by the somewhat lengthy discussion that took place on this topic at one of our leading foremen tailors' societies. The plan here given is both simple and reliable. It consists in adding on the quantity it is desired to lengthen it on the shoulder as per the shaded part, and then cut the back across as per the shaded part, and open out the pattern the same amount as has been added to the shoulder, and by this means the balance is preserved, then add on a little more spring at the hips. Of course it will be readily followed this will necessitate a new back, but we think that will be the most satisfactory plan of remedying this defect.

Too Loose at Top Button. Dia. 165.

This is often accompanied with looseness round the neck. The most ready method of altering this is to straighten the shoulder as illustrated on diagram 168. The last defect we shall note is in connection with sleeves, and shows itself in a series of

Creases across the Forearm of the Sleeve. Diagram 166.

The way to remedy this is to sink the forearm as per dotted lines, and if necessary lengthen it at the bottom. This, we think, closes the list of defects we can note in this work, which has already far exceeded the limits we had intended such a work to take.

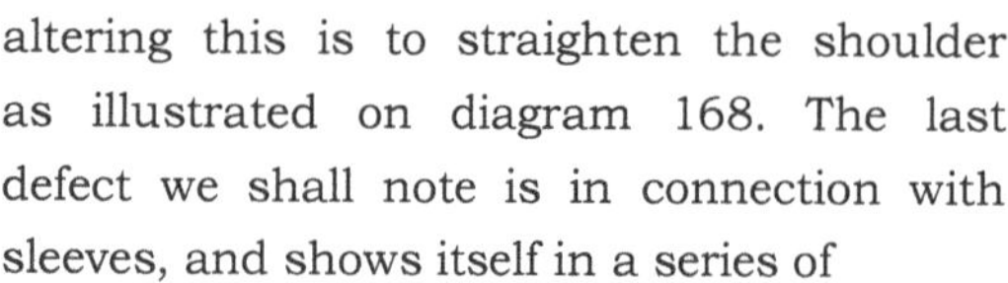

Economy

In order to make this work as complete as possible, we have added three diagrams of lays to give cutters an idea of what we consider economical cutting. Economy does not necessarily consist of getting a suit out of the least possible quantity, but rather taking it out of the cloth to the best advantage, leaving inlays where required, and placing the patterns down so that the material is not biased in any way.

Diagram 168.

This represents a Boy's Knicker Suit, 24 chest, cut out of 1⅛ yards, the facings are not large, but such is not generally of great importance. The patterns in every case used for these diagrams are the *Tailor and Cutter* Models.

This and the next diagram are taken from "Economy in Cutting", a work every cutter should possess; and as we have put it to an extended test in daily practice at the cutting board, we can speak somewhat authoritatively on its merits, which we believe to be of the highest order, and is a work that should be in the hands of every progressive cutter.

Diagram 169

This lay represents a Lounge Suit, 28 breast, 24 long, 37 sideseam, and is taken out of 1¾ yards, of 56 inch cloth. For smaller suits of the same type, the length required may be still further reduced by making the top and undersides of the trousers change, and putting seat pieces on, that is if the length of sleeves will admit of it, which they generally will in smaller sizes.

Diagram 170.

This lay represents a Lounge Jacket Suit, 32 breast, 26 long, 41 sideseam, and is taken out of 2¼ yards, 56 inch material. It is also suitable for sizes between 28 and 32 breast. A saving may be effected by putting top welts or top bands on the trousers which could be got between the sleeves and the undersides of trousers. It will be noticed that if a roll is required for the vest a small piece must be put on the forepart.

For larger sizes we must refer our readers to the work previously mentioned, and which may be obtained from the *Tailor and Cutter* Office, price 7s. 6d., or post free 7s. 9d.

THE ILLUSTRATIONS

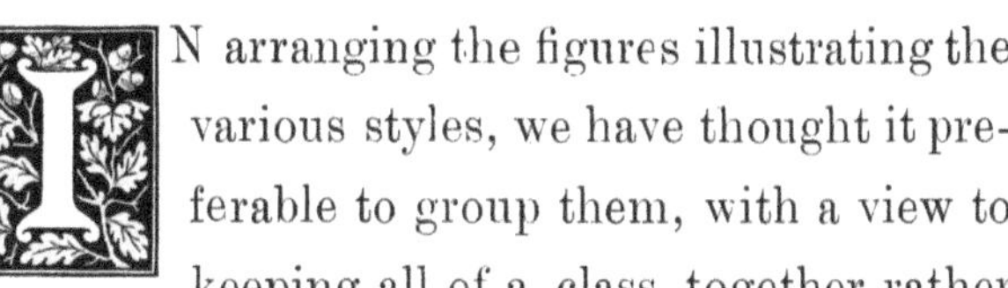

IN arranging the figures illustrating the various styles, we have thought it preferable to group them, with a view to keeping all of a class together rather than placing them in consecutive order, deeming they would be of the greatest service to our readers in that way, at the same time we have followed the consecutive order as near as possible, but making it of secondary importance. The shaded outline on Fig. 2 illustrates the development of corpulency, and which we feel sure will be very interesting to a large portion of our readers.

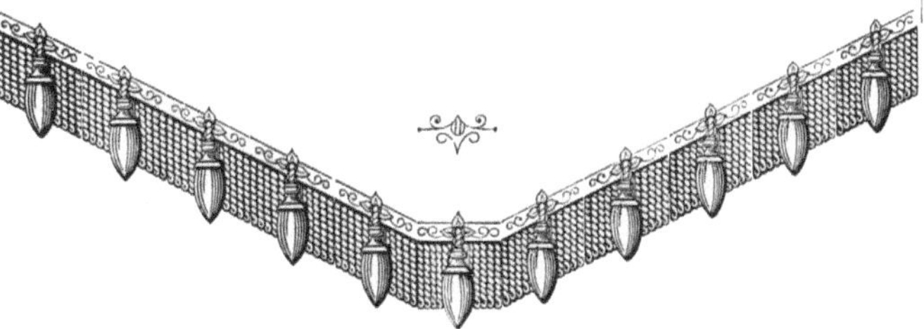

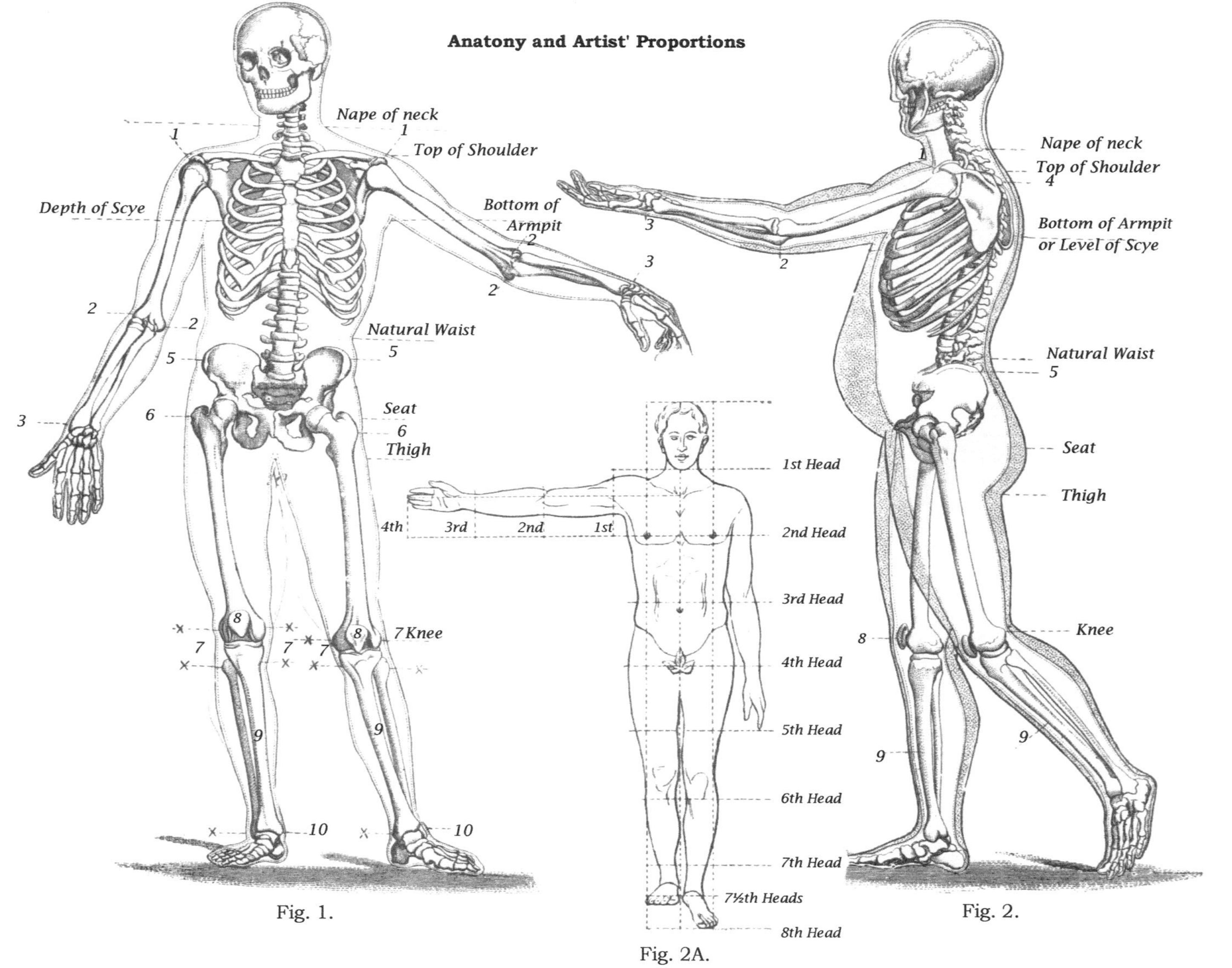

Anatony and Artist' Proportions
Nape of neck
Top of Shoulder
Depth of Scye
Bottom of Armpit
Natural Waist
Seat
Thigh
Knee
Nape of neck
Top of Shoulder
Bottom of Armpit or Level of Scye
Natural Waist
Seat
Thigh
Knee
1st Head
2nd Head
3rd Head
4th Head
5th Head
6th Head
7th Head
7½th Heads
8th Head
Fig. 1.
Fig. 2A.
Fig. 2.

Fig. 3.

Fig. 4.

Lounge, Fig. 7.

D.B. Reefer, Fig. 8.

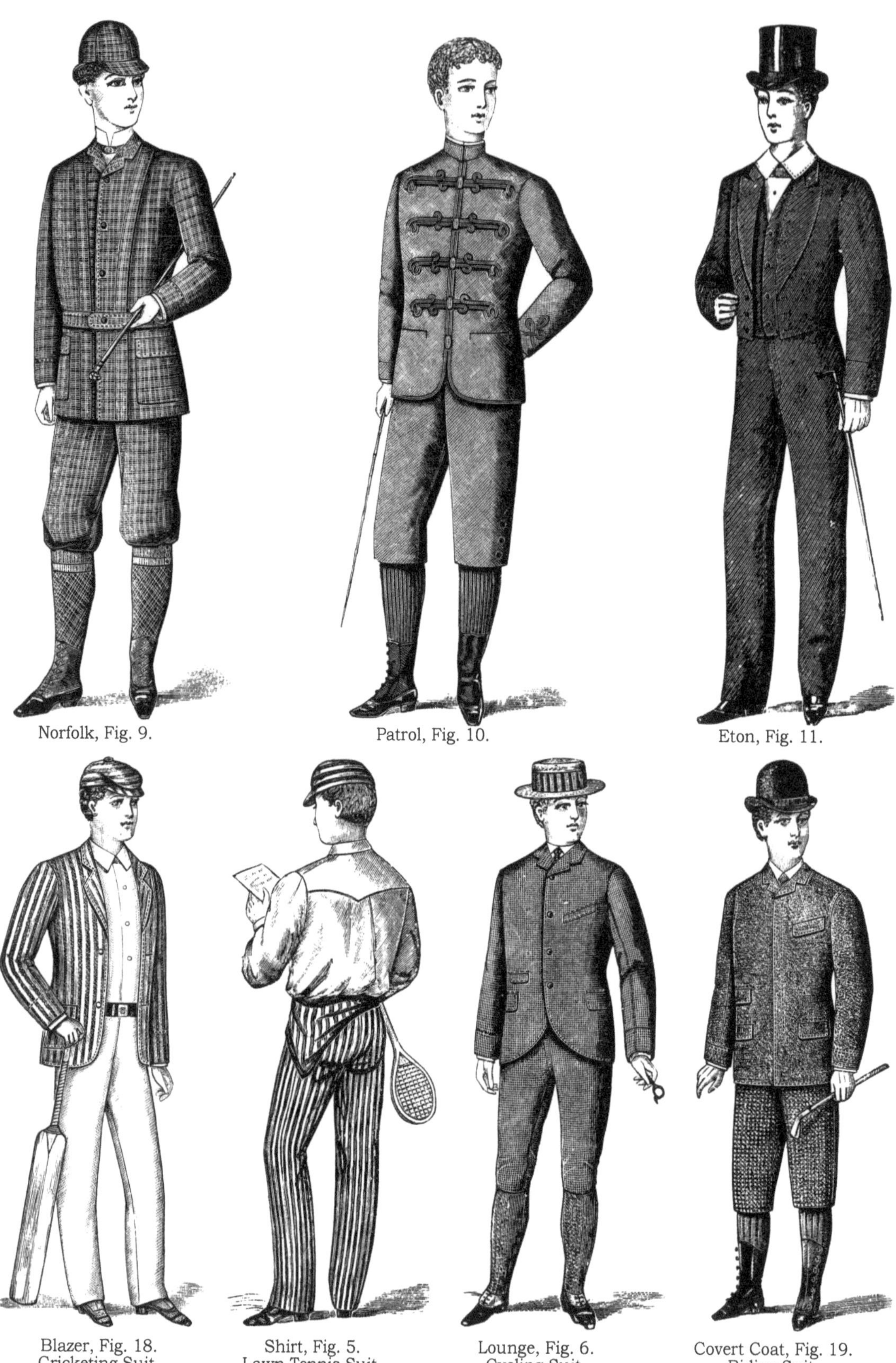

Norfolk, Fig. 9.

Patrol, Fig. 10.

Eton, Fig. 11.

Blazer, Fig. 18.
Cricketing Suit.

Shirt, Fig. 5.
Lawn Tennis Suit.

Lounge, Fig. 6.
Cycling Suit.

Covert Coat, Fig. 19.
Riding Suit.

Midshipman, Full Dress, Fig. 15.

Naval Cadet, Fig. 14.

Roll Collar Eton, Fig. 13.

D.B. Naval Round, Fig. 12.

Dress Coat, Fig. 17.

Morning Coat, Fig. 16.

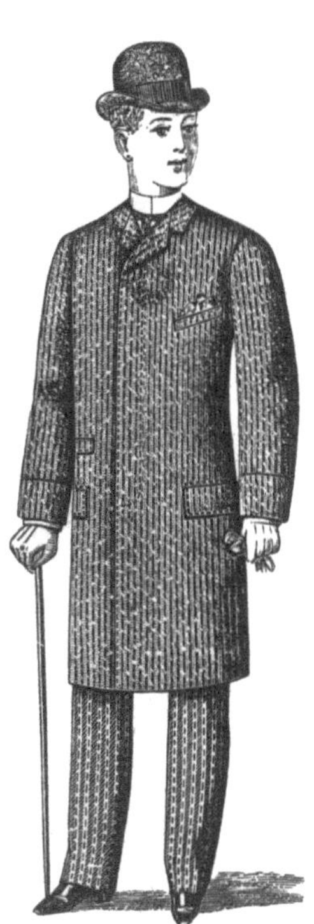

Fly-front Overcoat, Fig. 20.

S B. Overcoat, Fig. 21.

D.B. Overcoat, Fig. 22.   Ulster and Cape, Fig. 23.   Inverness, Fig. 24.   Invernes, Fig. 28.

Pyjama Suit, Fig. 39.   Dressing Gown, Fig. 26.   Cassock, Fig. 27.   Chorister's Surplice, Fig. 28.

Page's Suit, Fig. 29.

Groom's Suit, Fig. 30.

D.B. Reefer, Fig. 54.

Jockey Suit, Fig. 40.

Sailor Blouse, Fig. 51.

Kilt Frock, Fig. 52.

Jack Tar Suit, Fig. 53.

Girl's Kilt Frock, Fig. 52a.

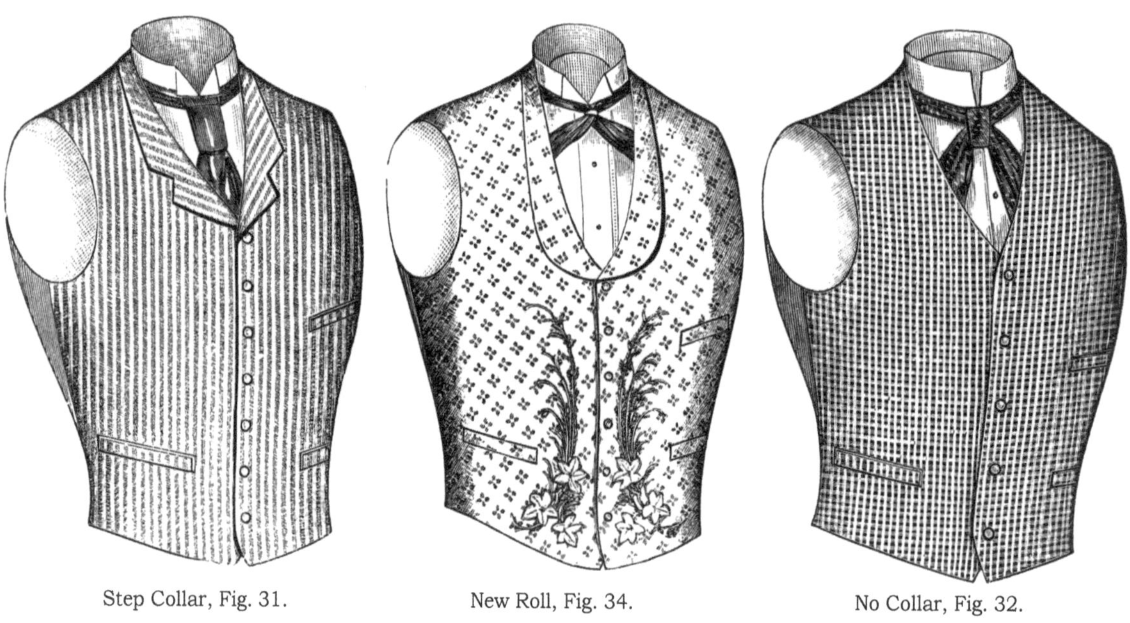

Step Collar, Fig. 31.　　　New Roll, Fig. 34.　　　No Collar, Fig. 32.

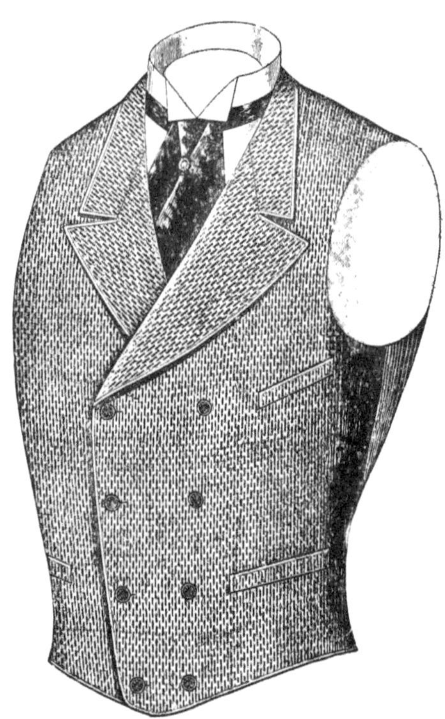

D.B. Vest, Fig. 37.

Sleeve Vest, Fig. 38.

Step Stand, Fig. 33.

Dress Vest, Fig. 35.

Roll, Fig. 36.

The Court, Fig. 48.

The Monte Carlo, Fig. 59.

The Highland, Fig. 41.   Little Lord Faunterloy, Fig. 63.

The Prince, Fig. 42.

The Count, Fig. 43.

The Duke, Fig. 44.

The Rifle, Fig. 45.

The Gordon, Fig. 46.

The Artilleur, Fig. 47.

The Lancer, Fig. 49.

The Regent, Fig. 50.

The Norfolk, Fig. 55.

The Brighton, Fig. 57.

The New York, Fig. 56.

The Sydenham, Fig. 58.

The Austrian, Fig. 62.

The Kilt Overcoat, Fig. 61.

The Scarborough, Fig. 60.

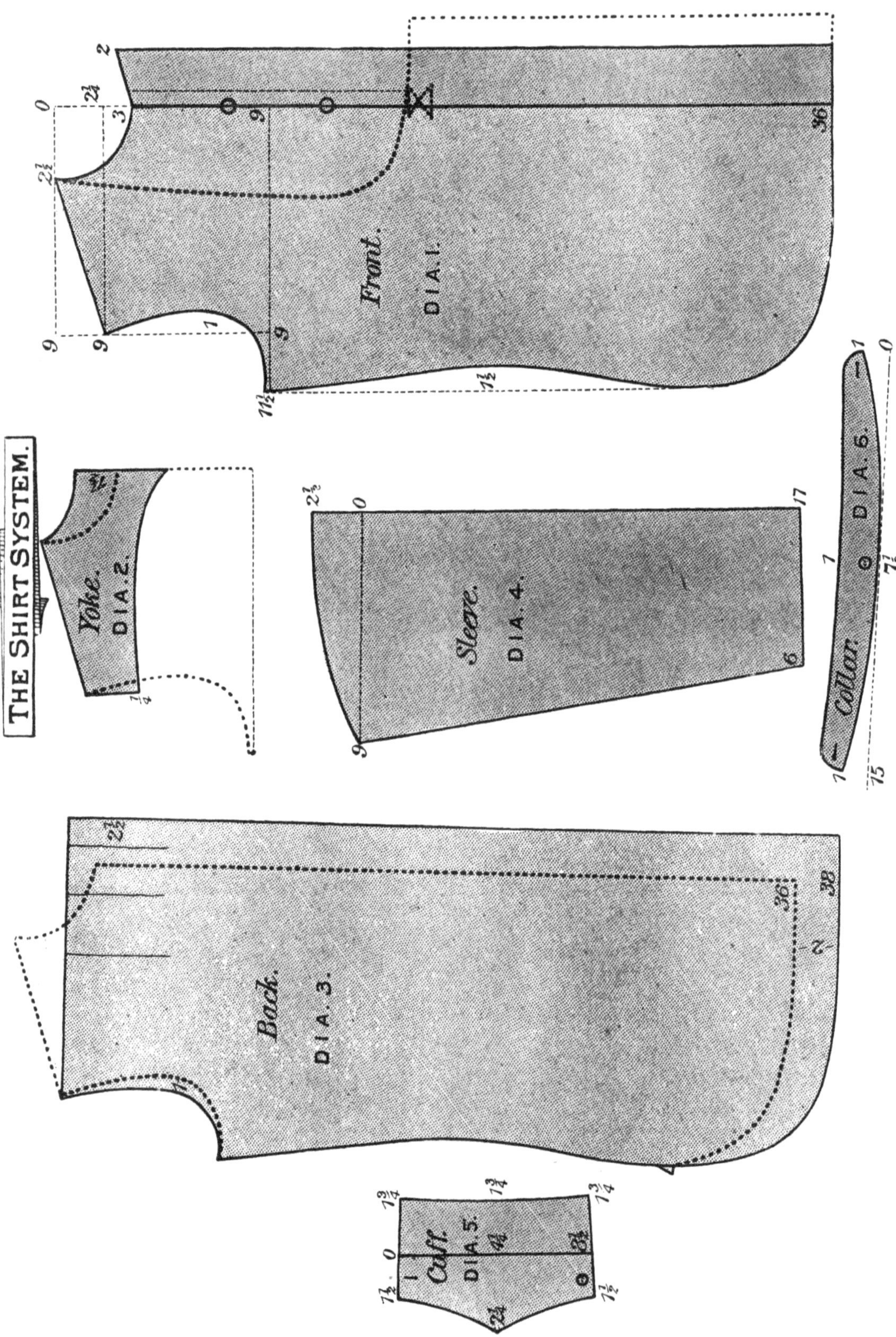
THE SHIRT SYSTEM.
Front.
DIA. 1.
Yoke.
DIA. 2.
Sleeve.
DIA. 4.
Collar.
DIA. 6.
Back.
DIA. 3.
Cuff.
DIA. 5.

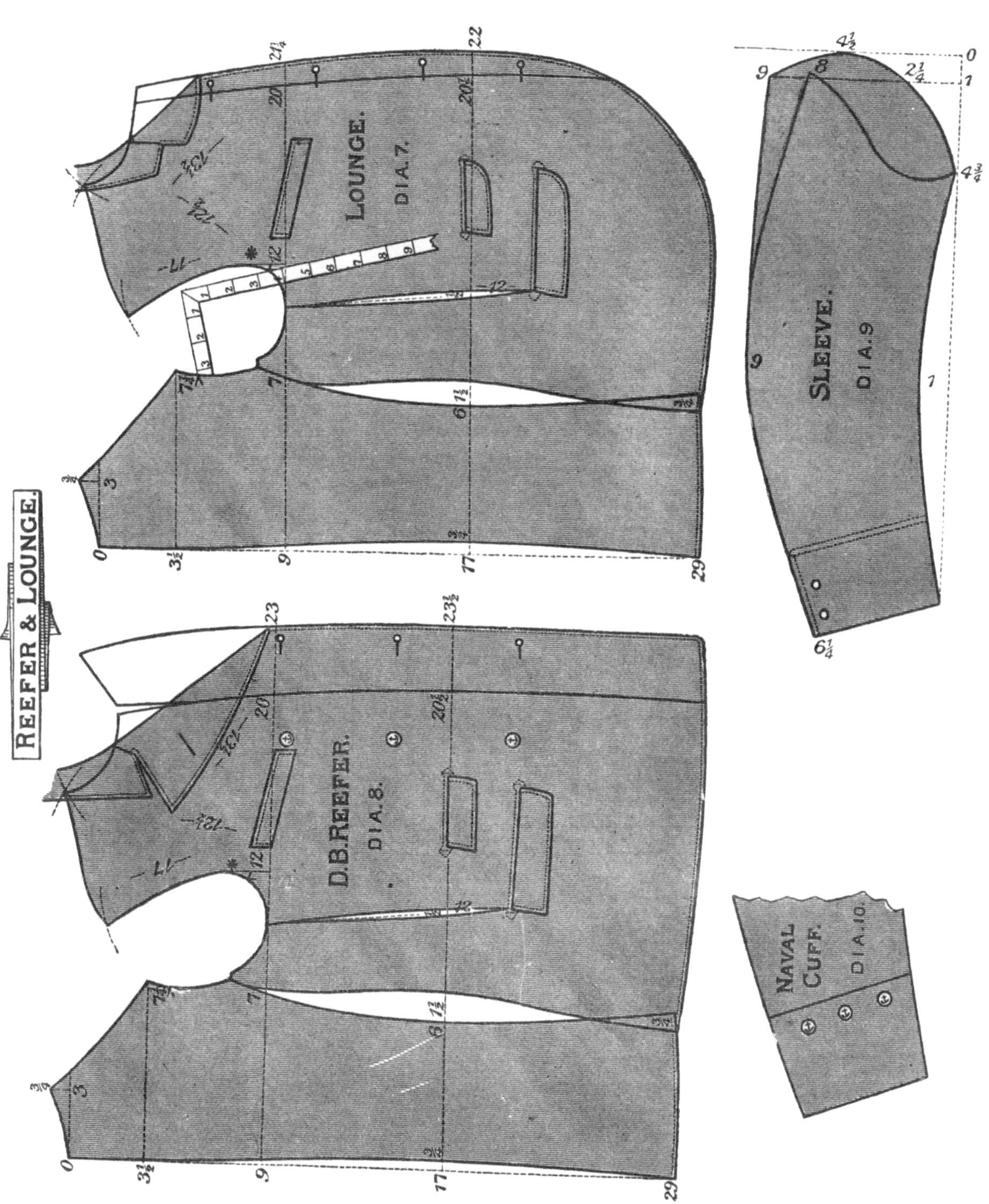

REEFER & LOUNGE.
LOUNGE.
DIA. 7.
D.B. REEFER.
DIA. 8.
SLEEVE.
DIA. 9.
NAVAL CUFF.
DIA. 10.

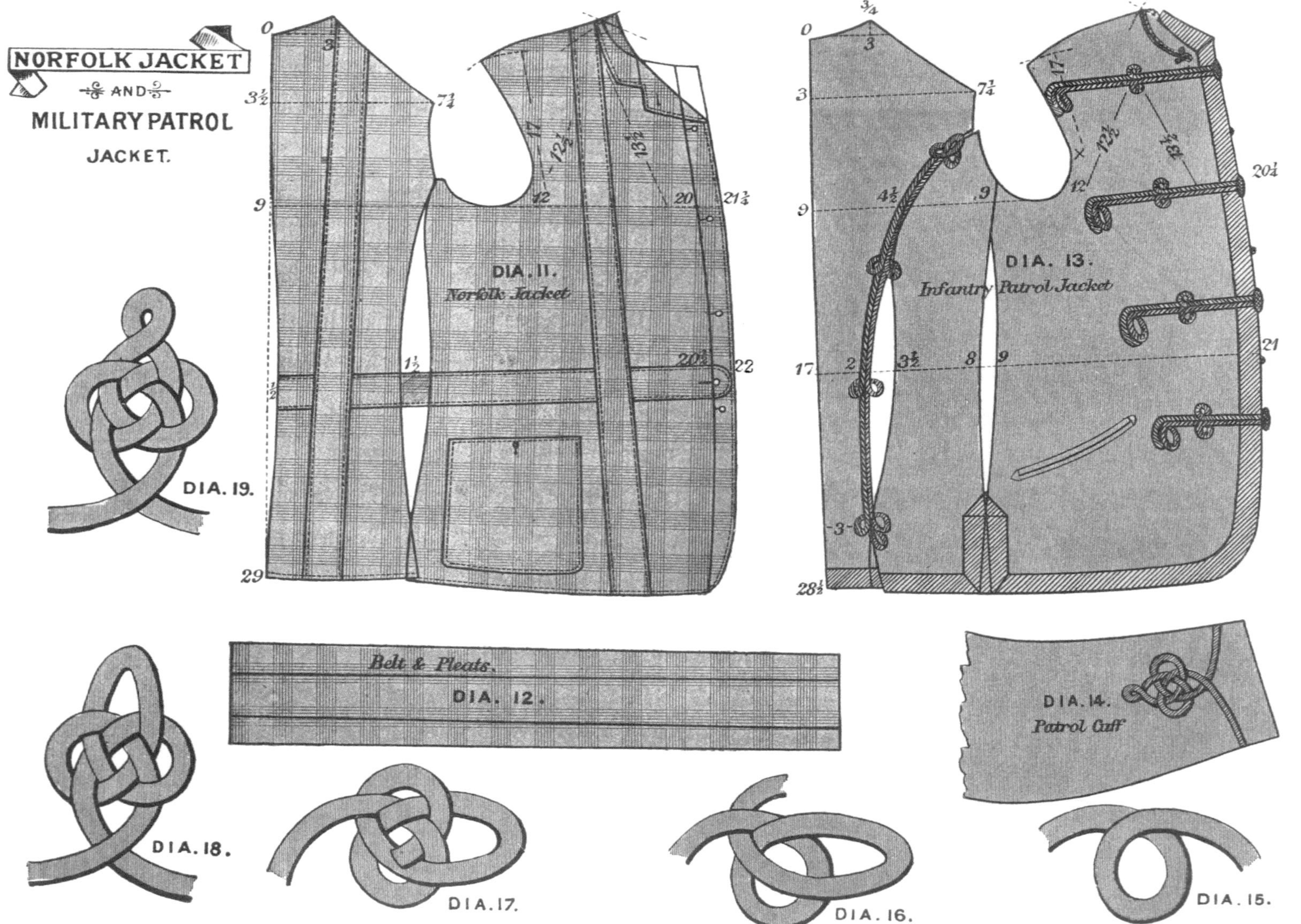
NORFOLK JACKET
AND
MILITARY PATROL
JACKET.
DIA. 11. Norfolk Jacket
DIA. 12. Belt & Pleats.
DIA. 13. Infantry Patrol Jacket
DIA. 14. Patrol Cuff
DIA. 15.
DIA. 16.
DIA. 17.
DIA. 18.
DIA. 19.

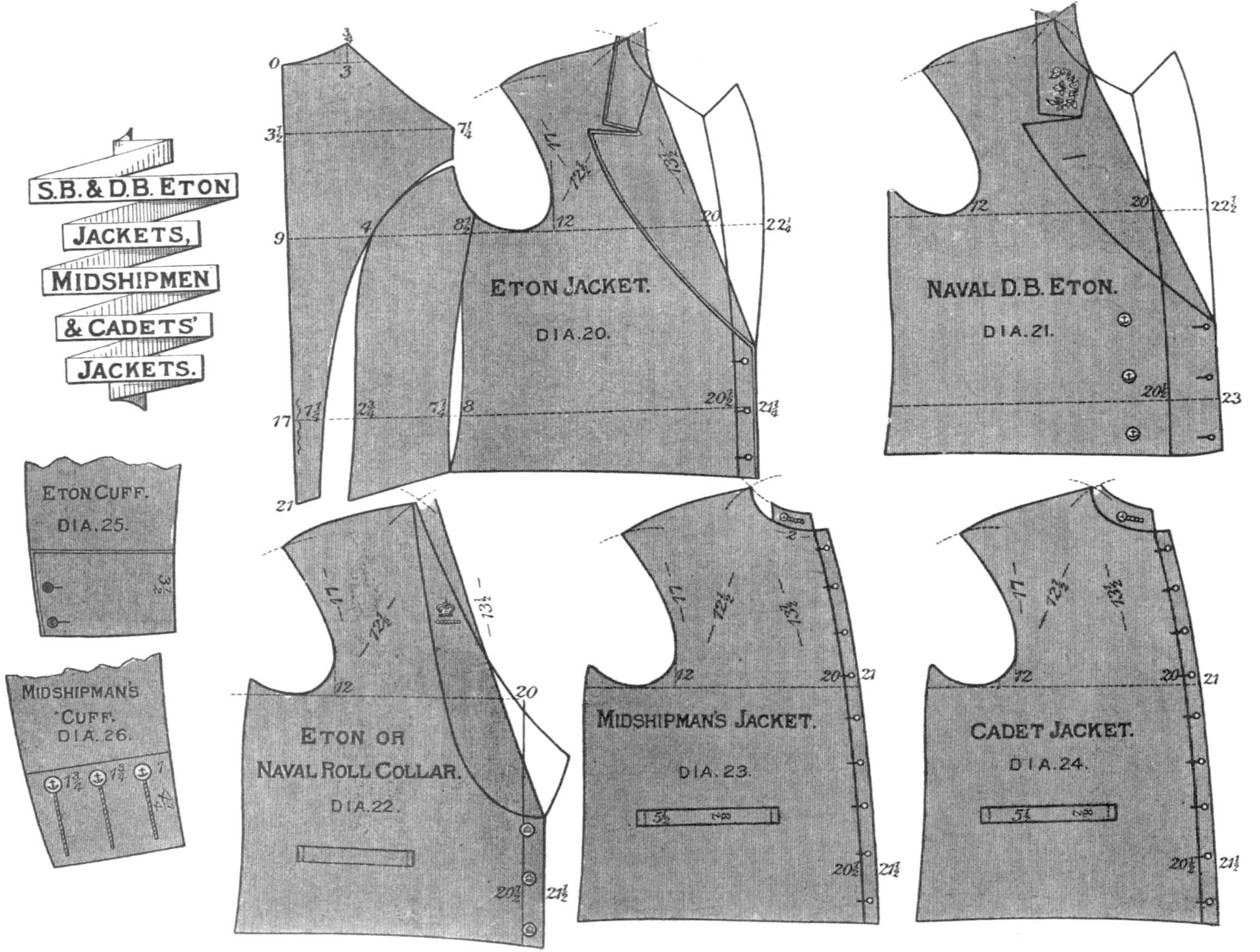
S.B. & D.B. ETON
JACKETS,
MIDSHIPMEN
& CADETS'
JACKETS.
ETON CUFF.
DIA.25.
MIDSHIPMAN'S
CUFF.
DIA.26.
ETON JACKET.
DIA.20.
NAVAL D.B. ETON.
DIA.21.
ETON OR
NAVAL ROLL COLLAR.
DIA.22.
MIDSHIPMAN'S JACKET.
DIA.23.
CADET JACKET.
DIA.24.

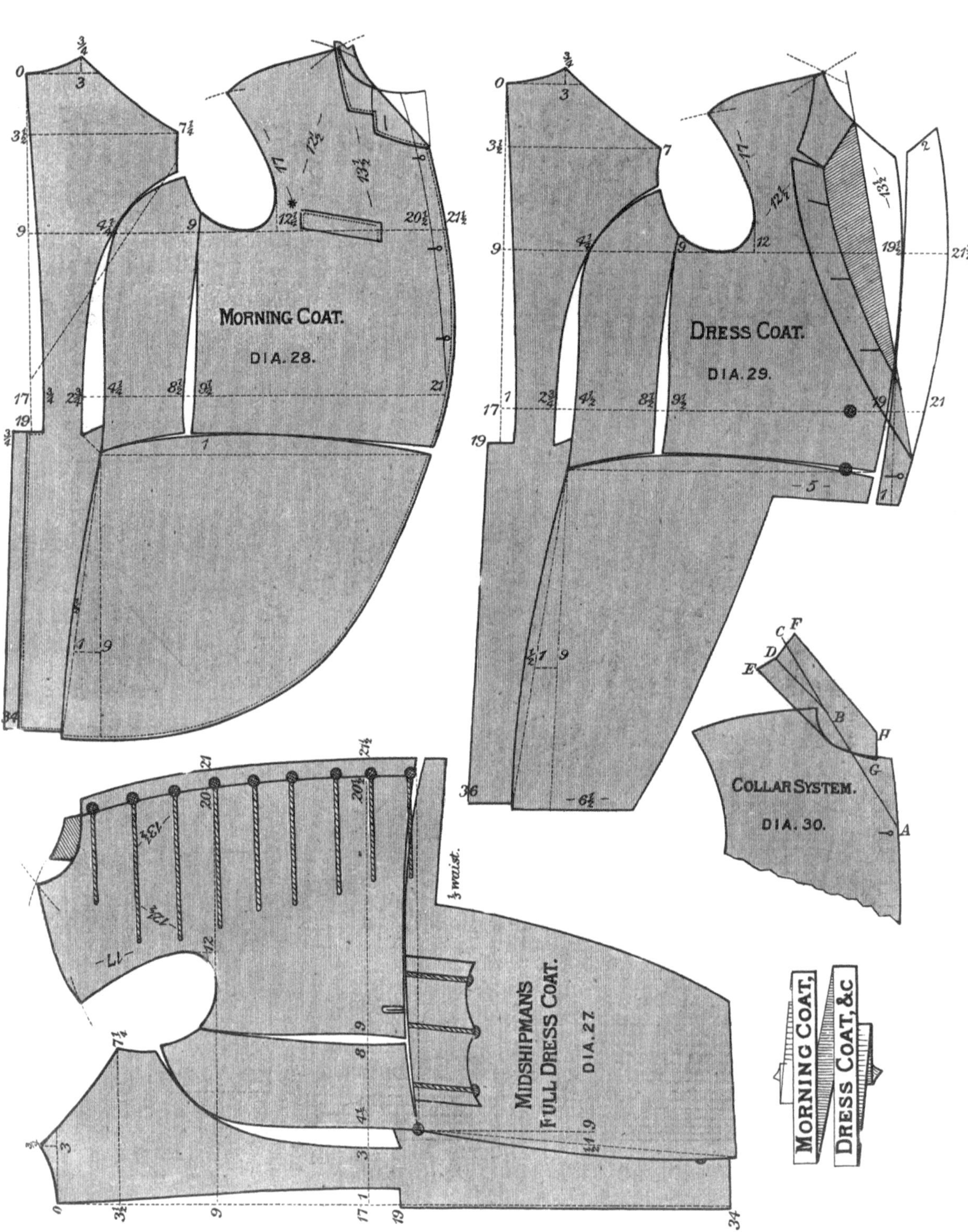
MORNING COAT.
DIA. 28.
DRESS COAT.
DIA. 29.
COLLAR SYSTEM.
DIA. 30.
MIDSHIPMANS FULL DRESS COAT.
DIA. 27.
MORNING COAT,
DRESS COAT, &c

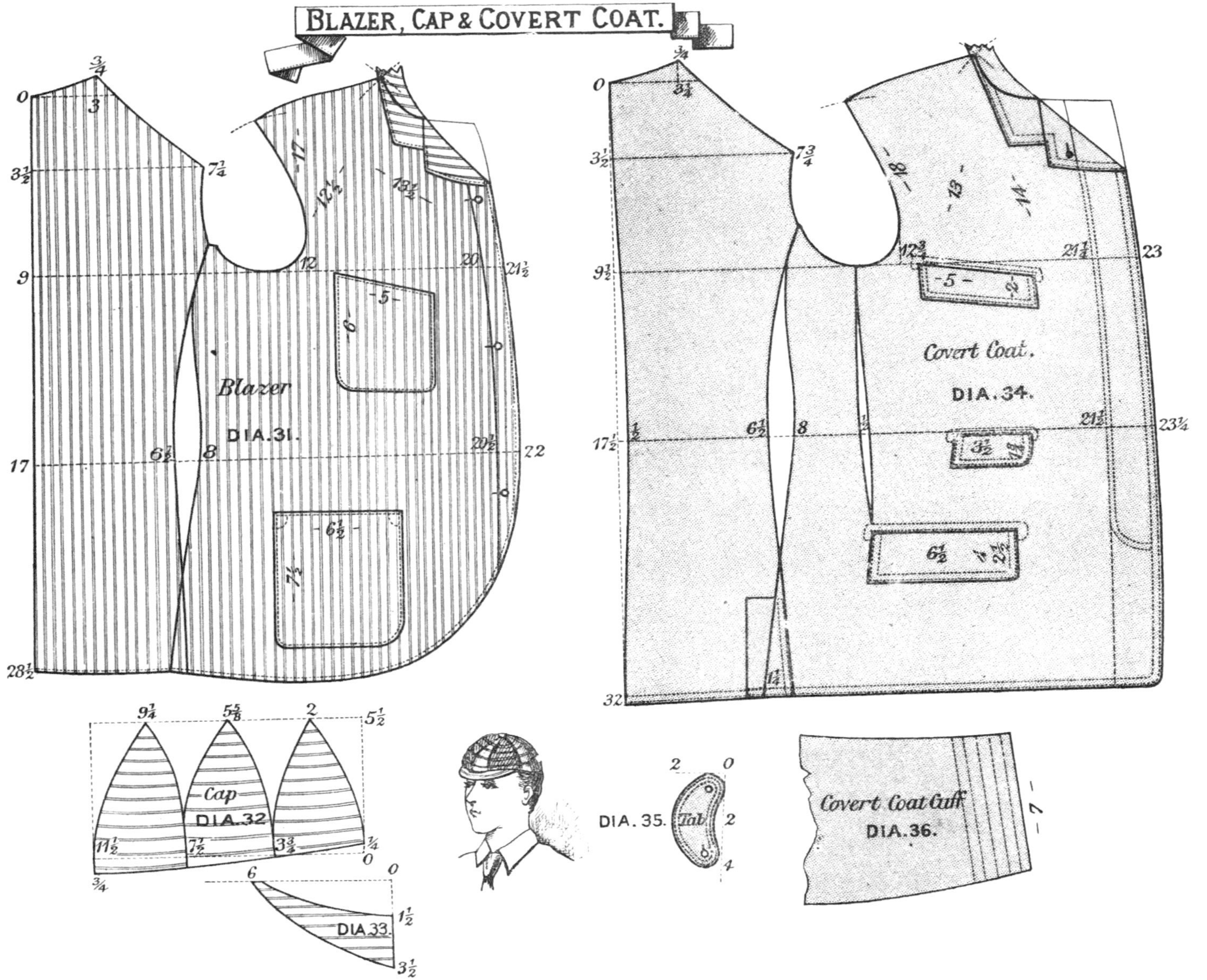

BLAZER, CAP & COVERT COAT.
Blazer
DIA. 31.
Covert Coat.
DIA. 34.
Cap
DIA. 32.
DIA. 33.
DIA. 35.
Tab.
Covert Coat Cuff
DIA. 36.

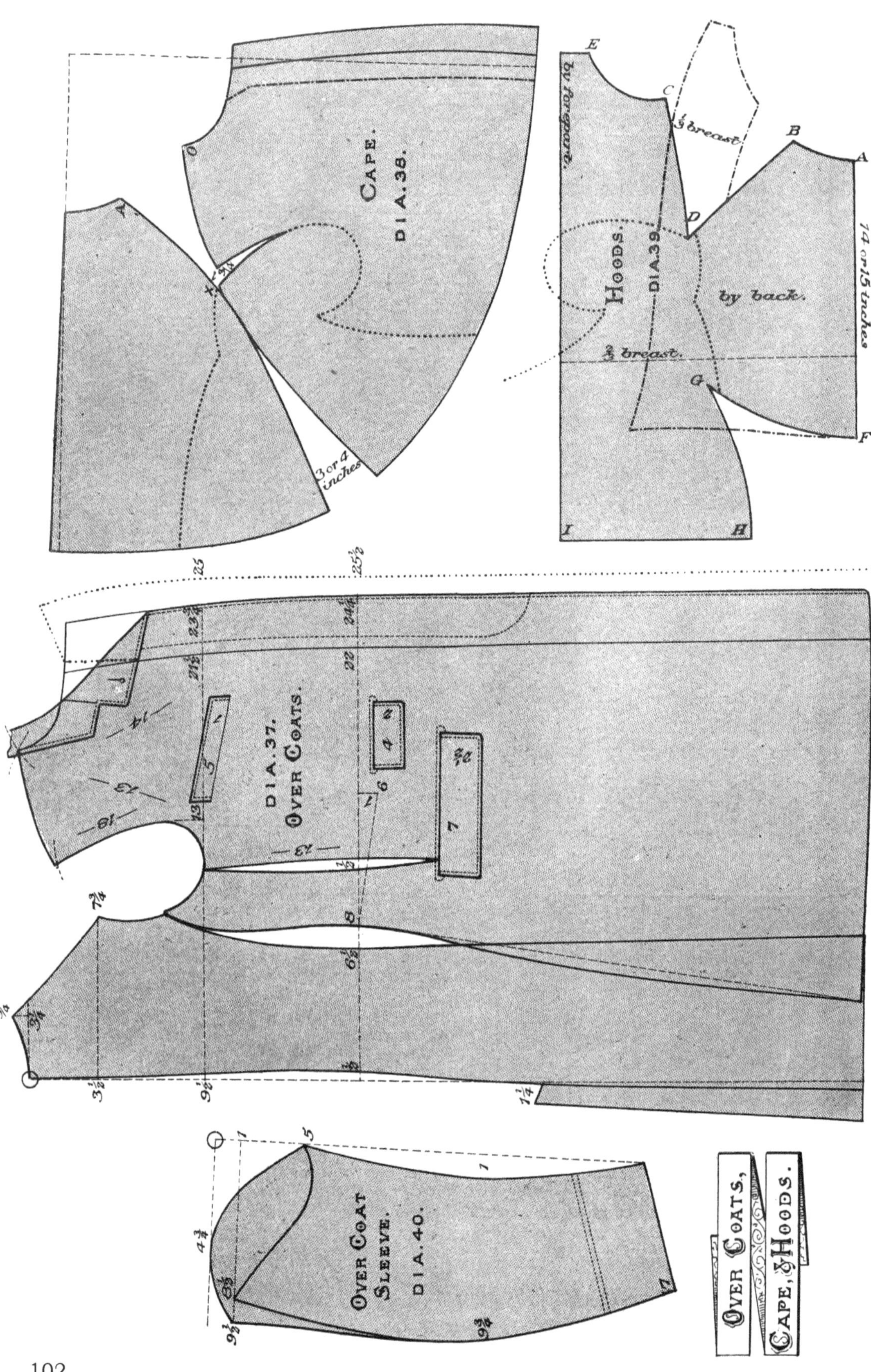
Cape.
Dia. 38.
Hoods.
Dia. 39.
by foregart.
by back.
breast
½ breast
14 or 15 inches
3 or 4 inches
Dia. 37.
Over Coats.
Over Coat
Sleeve.
Dia. 40.
Over Coats,
Cape, & Hoods.

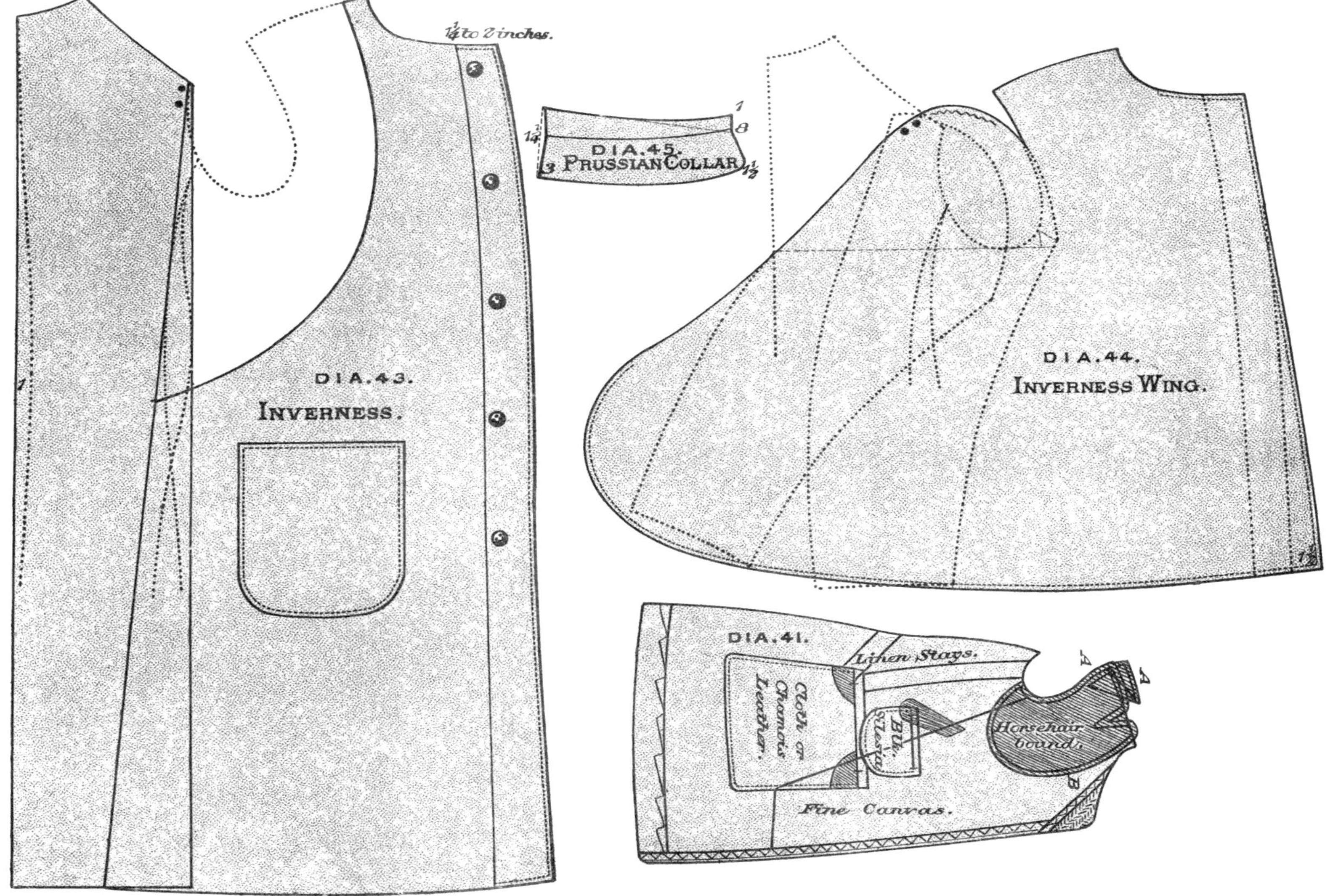
¼ to 2 inches.
DIA. 45.
3 PRUSSIAN COLLAR
DIA. 43.
INVERNESS.
DIA. 44.
INVERNESS WING.
DIA. 41.
Linen Stays.
Cloth or Chamois Leather.
Blk. Silesia
Fine Canvas.
Horsehair Cloth
A
A
B

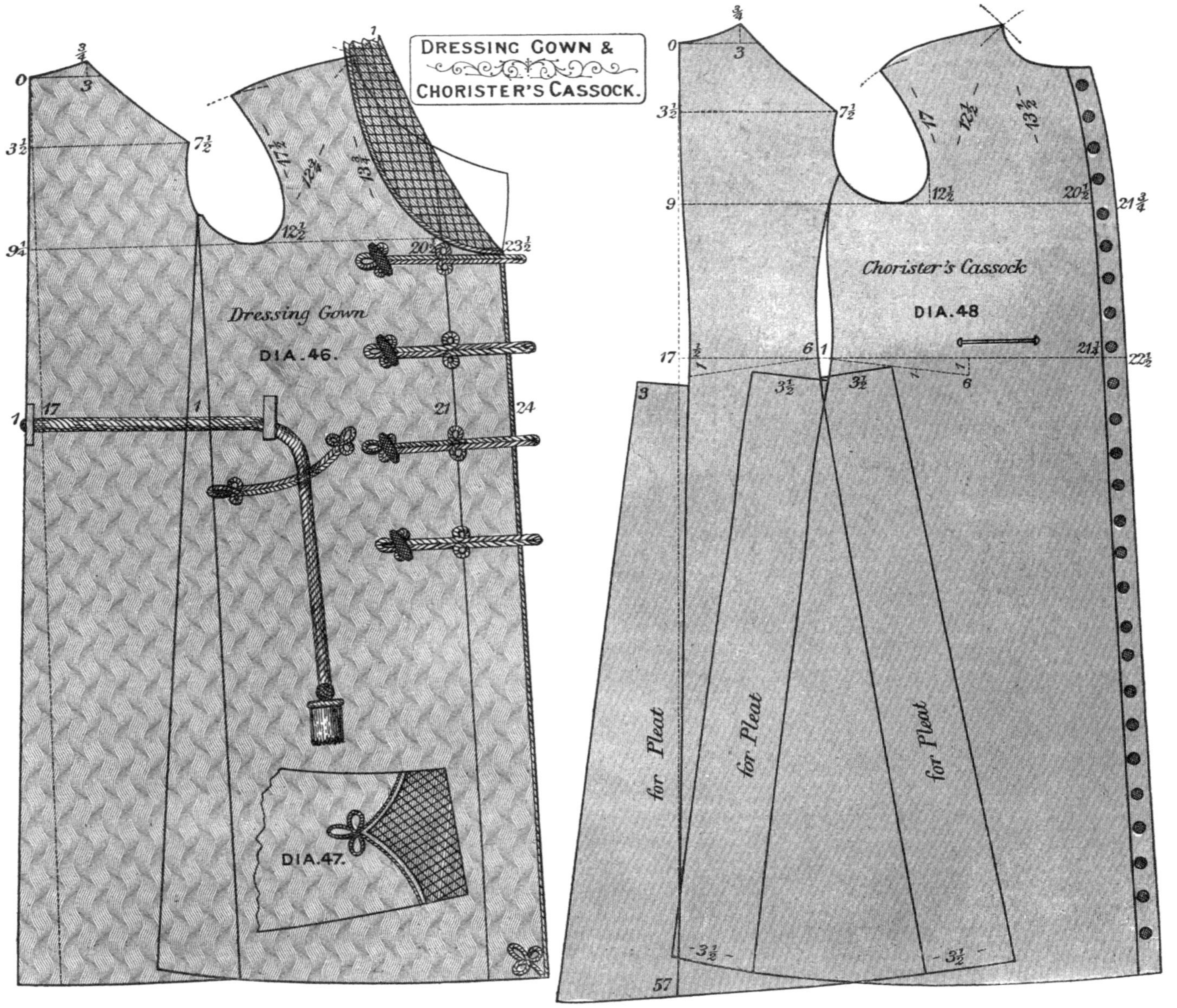

DRESSING GOWN &
CHORISTER'S CASSOCK.
Dressing Gown
DIA. 46.
DIA. 47.
Chorister's Cassock
DIA. 48
for Pleat
for Pleat
for Pleat

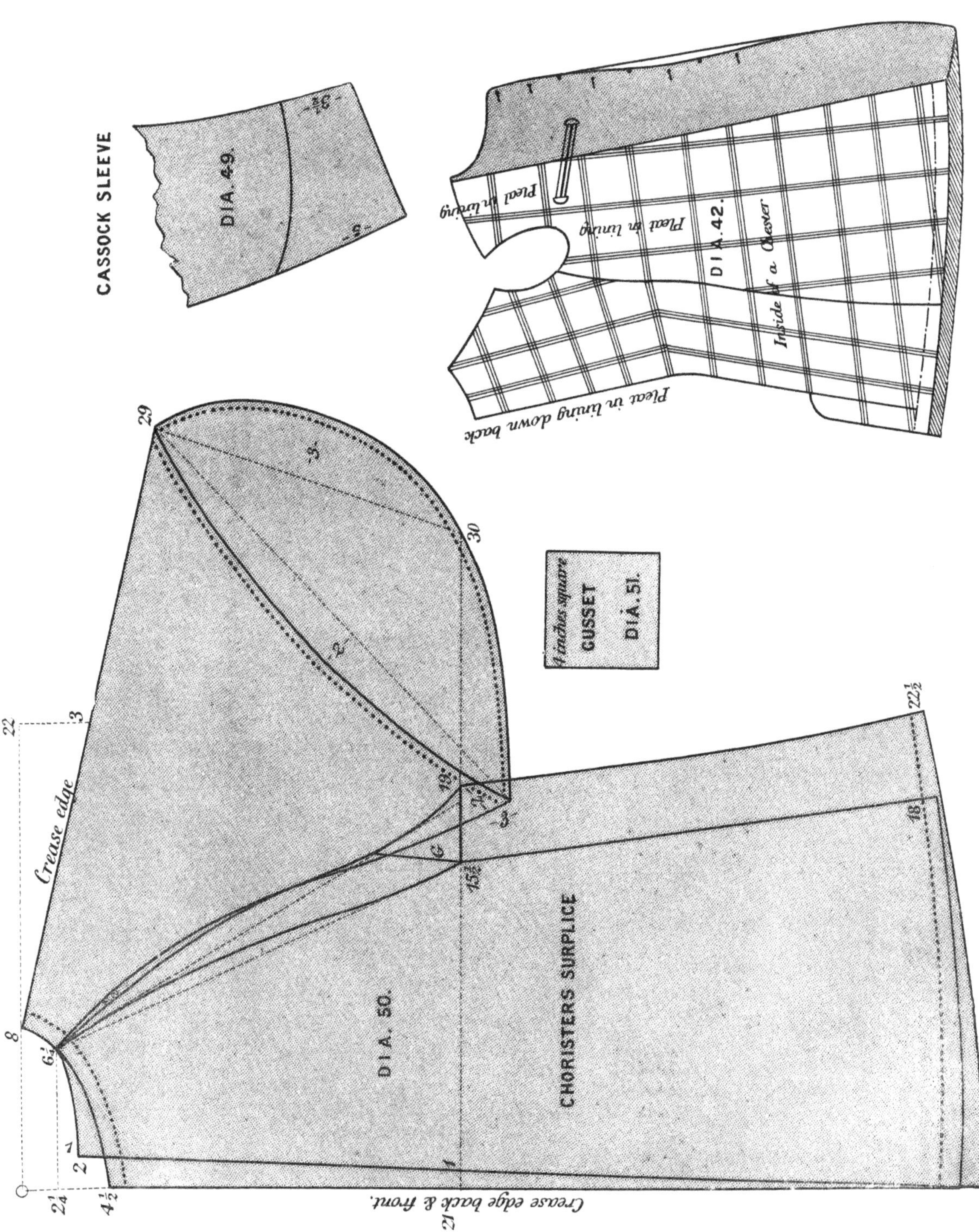

CASSOCK SLEEVE
DIA. 49.
DIA. 42.
Pleat in lining
Pleat in lining
Inside of a Cassock
Pleat in lining down back
29
30
5
2
3
6
GUSSET
DIA. 51.
7 inches square
DIA. 50.
CHORISTERS SURPLICE
Crease edge
Crease edge back & front.
22
3
8
6¼
1
2
2¼
4½
22½
18

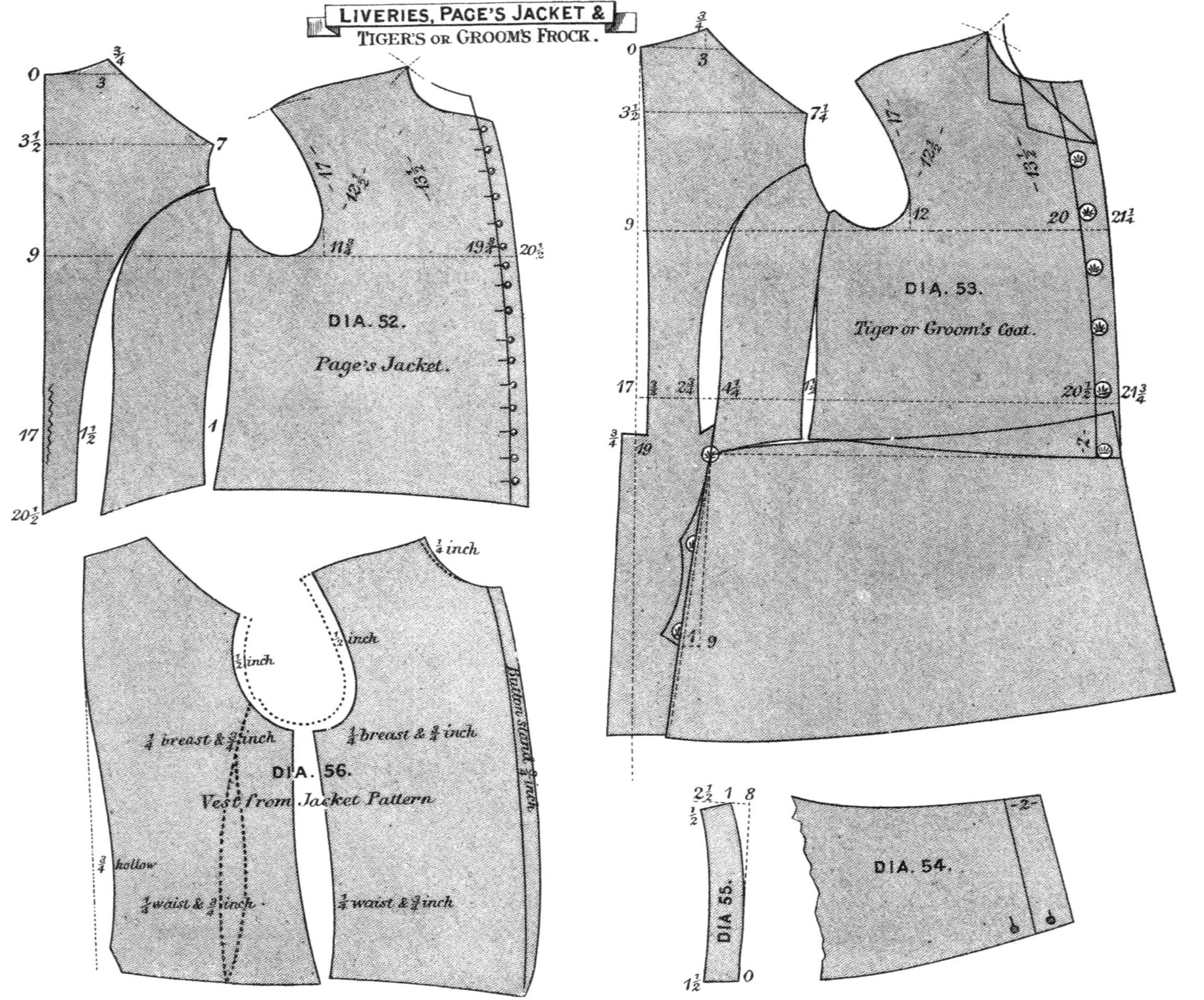

LIVERIES, PAGE'S JACKET &
TIGER'S OR GROOM'S FROCK.
DIA. 52.
Page's Jacket.
DIA. 53.
Tiger or Groom's Coat.
DIA. 56.
Vest from Jacket Pattern
¼ breast & ¾ inch
¼ breast & ¾ inch
¼ waist & ¾ inch
¼ waist & ¾ inch
hollow
¼ inch
½ inch
½ inch
Button stand ¾ inch
DIA. 55.
DIA. 54.

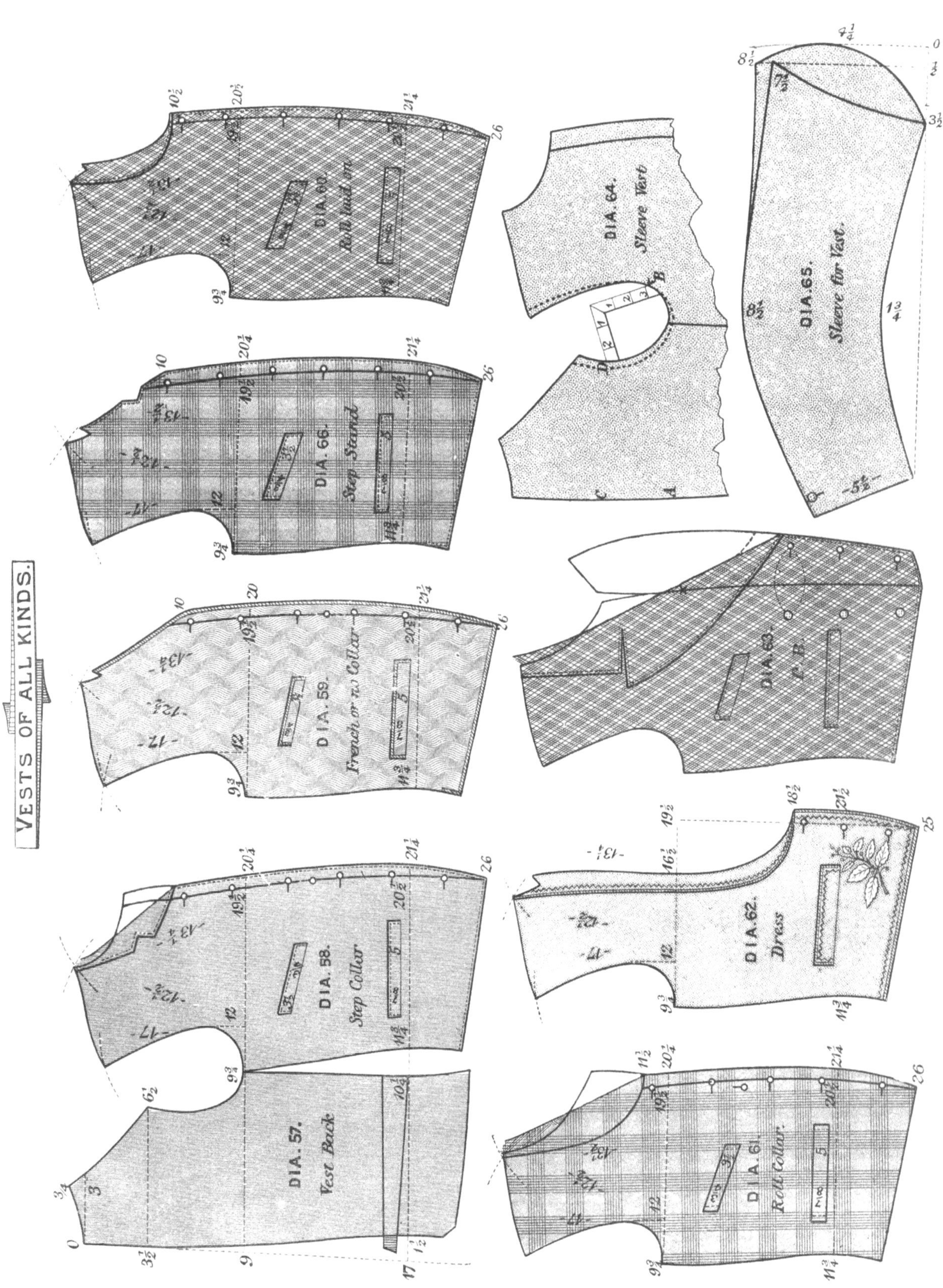
VESTS OF ALL KINDS.
DIA. 60.
Roll Collar
DIA. 66.
Step Stand
DIA. 59.
French or ½ Collar
DIA. 58.
Step Collar
DIA. 57.
Vest Back
DIA. 64.
Sleeve Vest
DIA. 65.
Sleeve for Vest.
DIA. 63.
L. B.
DIA. 62.
Dress
DIA. 61.
Roll Collar.

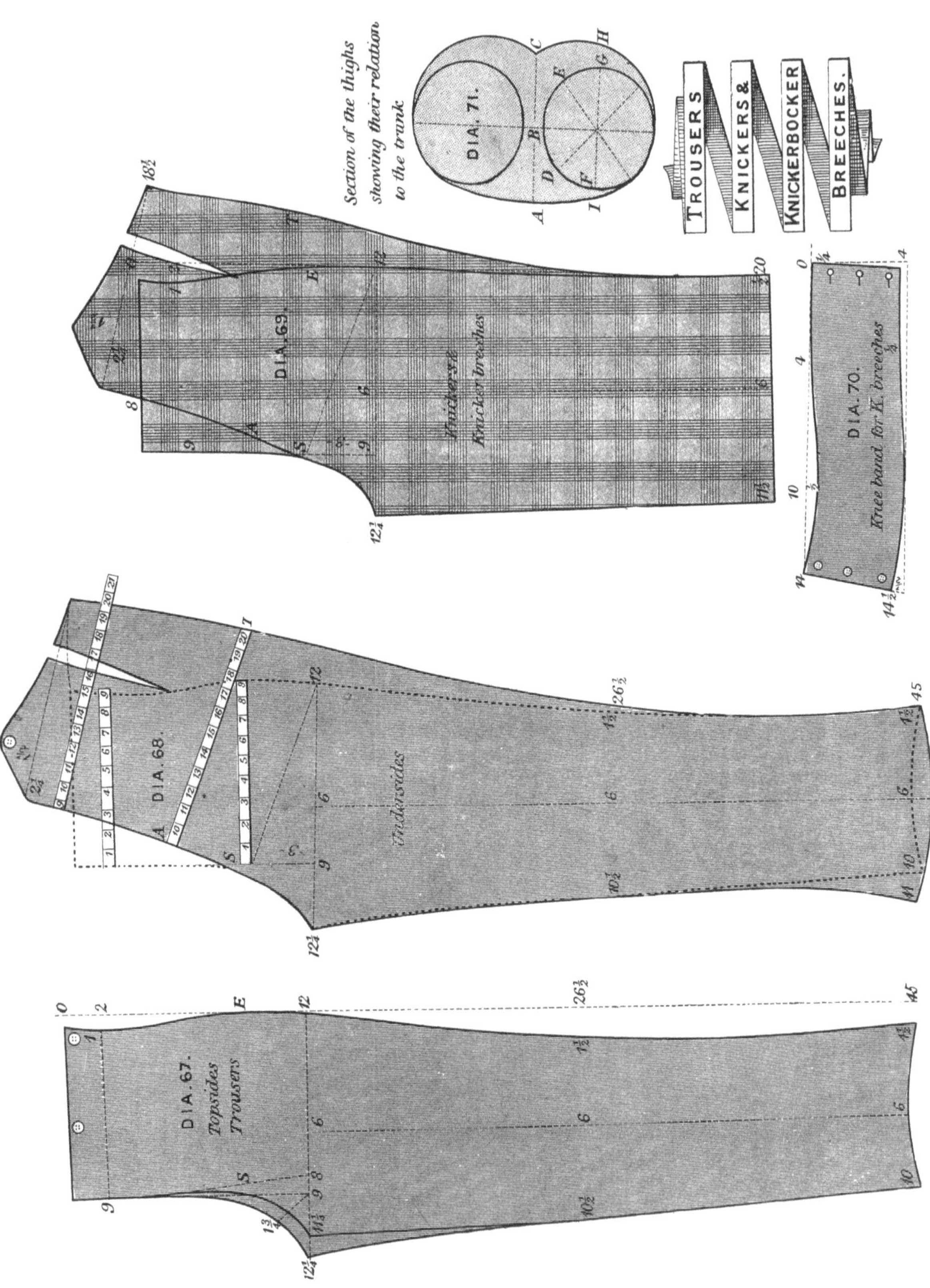

Section of the thighs showing their relation to the trunk
DIA. 71.
C
H
G
E
B
F
A
D
I
TROUSERS
KNICKERS &
KNICKERBOCKER
BREECHES.
18½
DIA. 69.
Knickers &
Knicker breeches
20
12¼
DIA. 70.
Knee band for K. breeches
0
¼
¼
4
10
14
14½
20 21
DIA. 68.
Undersides
26½
1½
45
1½
6
6
40
12¼
10½
0
2
E
12
DIA. 67.
Topsides
Trousers
26½
45
1½
6
6
40
10½
9
12¼

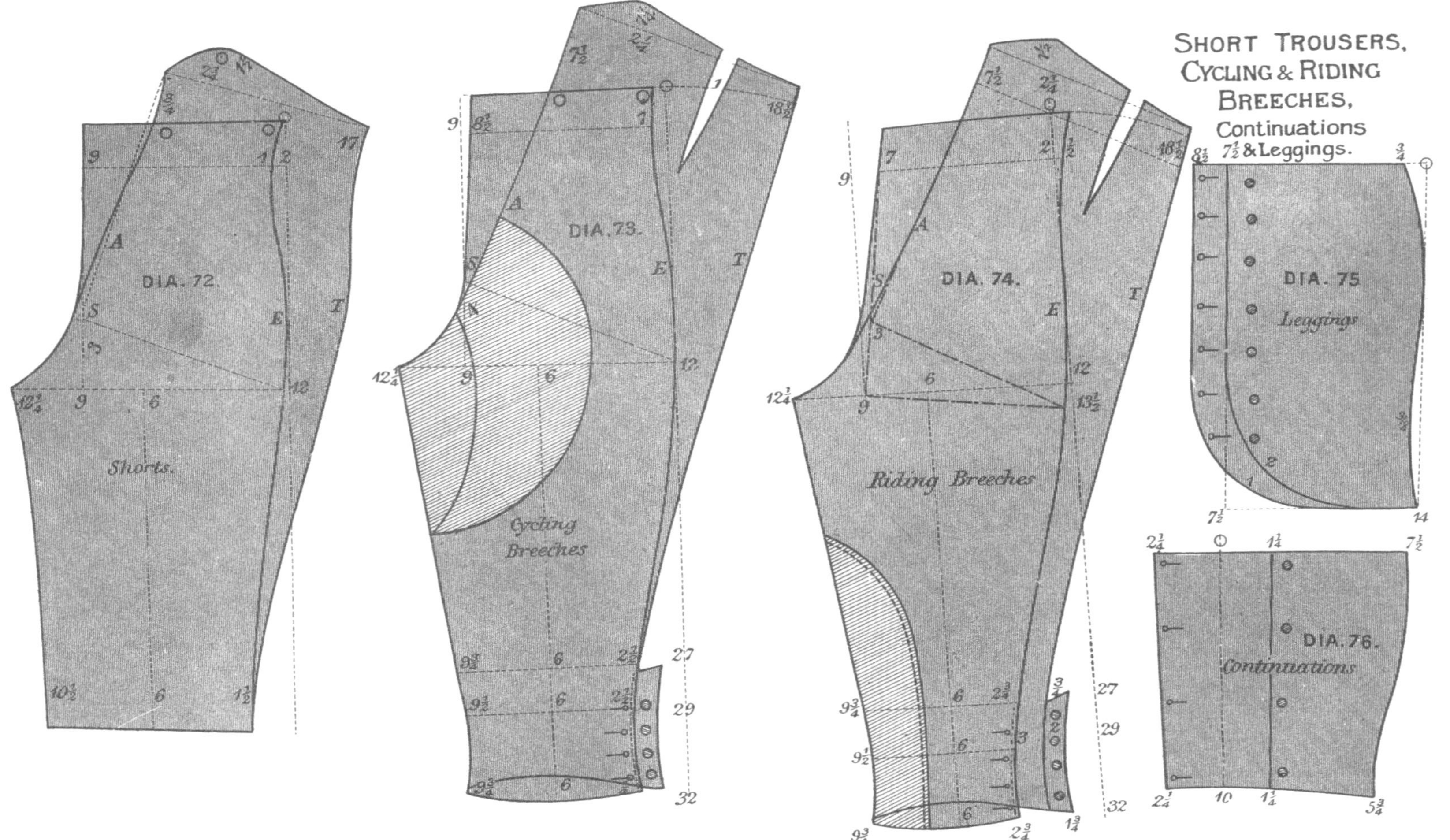
SHORT TROUSERS,
CYCLING & RIDING
BREECHES,
Continuations
7½ & Leggings.
DIA. 72.
Shorts.
DIA. 73.
Cycling Breeches
DIA. 74.
Riding Breeches
DIA. 75
Leggings
DIA. 76.
Continuations

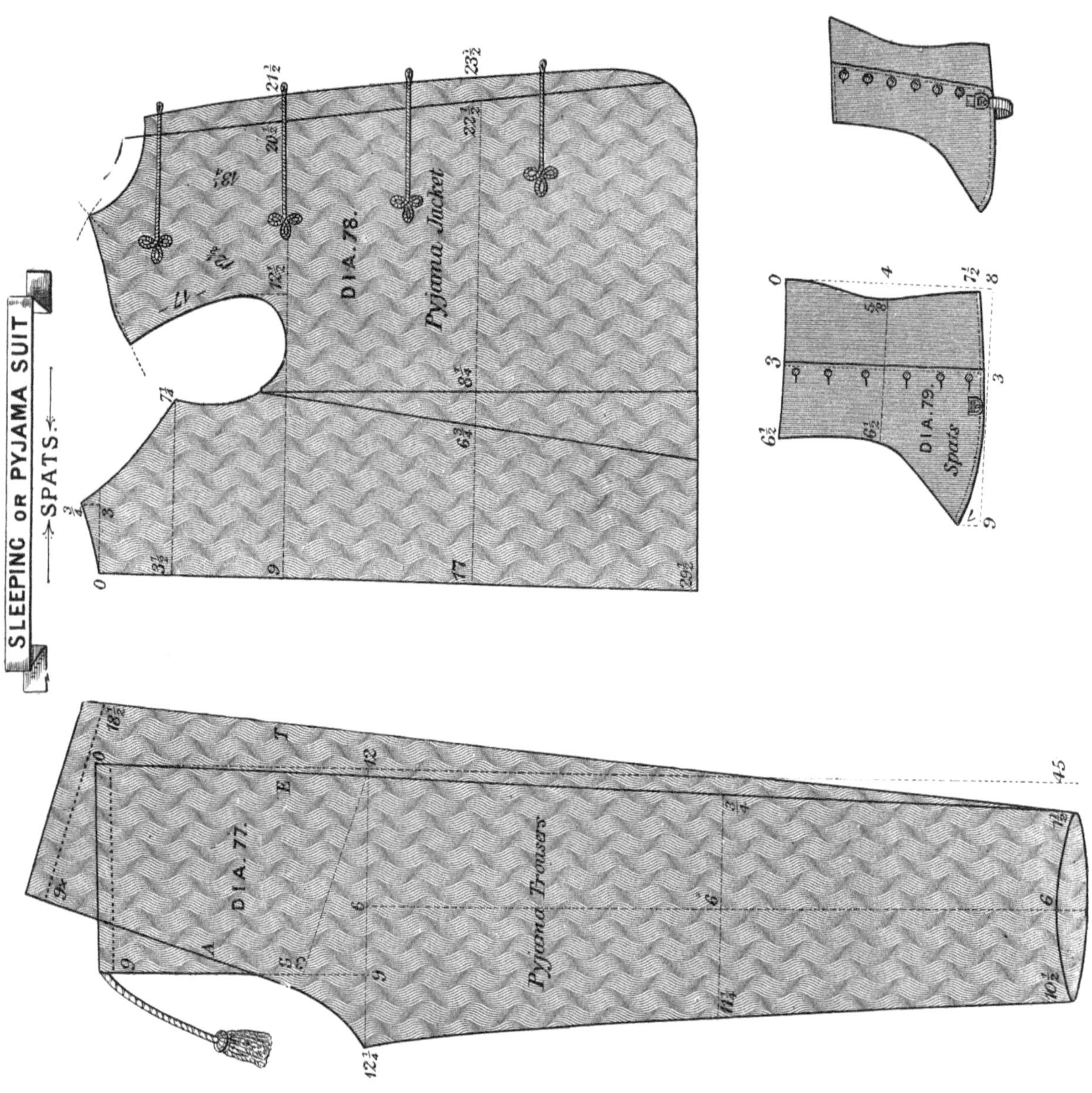

SLEEPING OR PYJAMA SUIT
SPATS.
DIA. 78.
Pyjama Jacket.
DIA. 79.
Spats
DIA. 77.
Pyjama Trousers

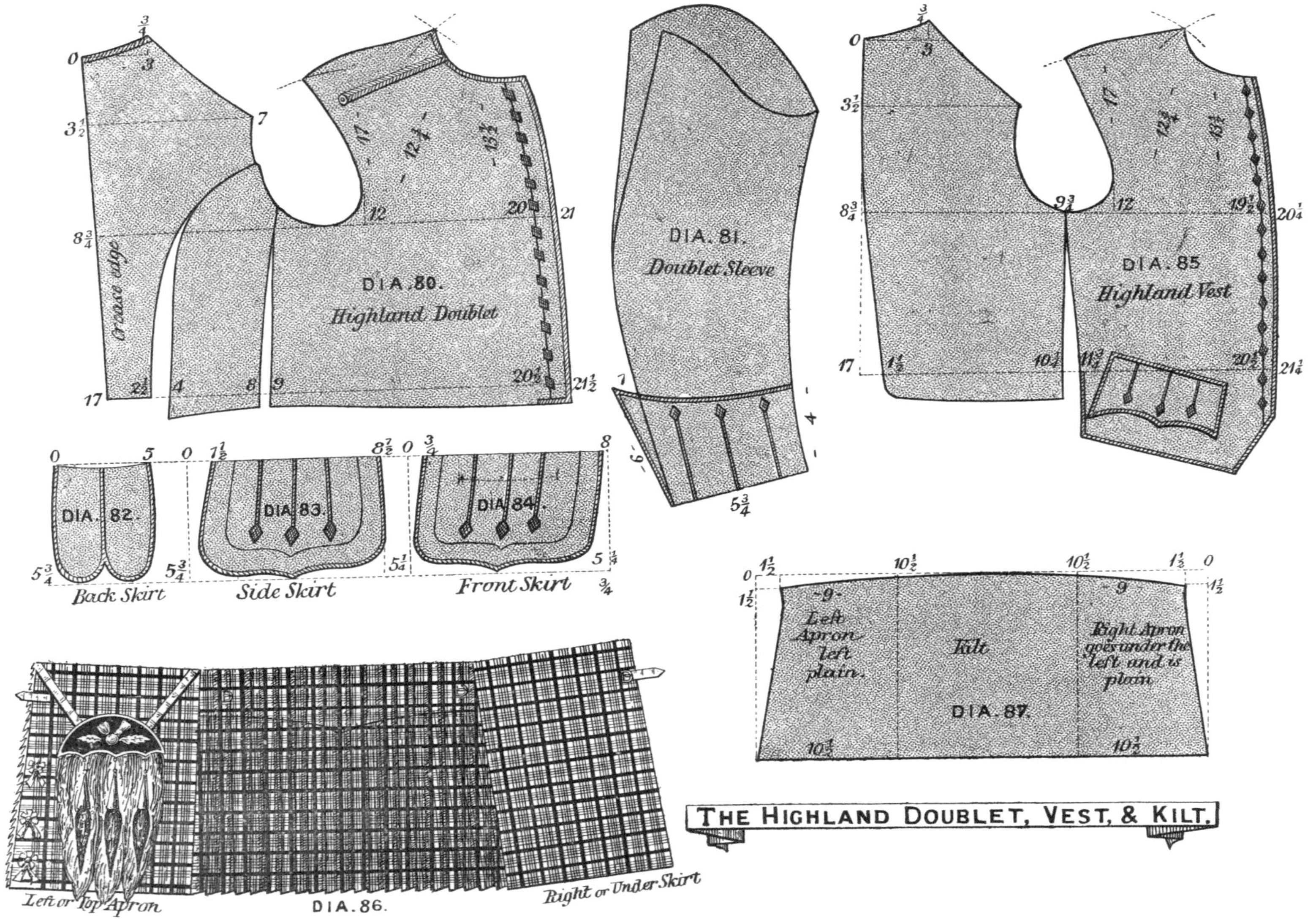

DIA. 80.
Highland Doublet
Crease edge
DIA. 81.
Doublet Sleeve
DIA. 85
Highland Vest
DIA. 82.
Back Skirt
DIA. 83.
Side Skirt
DIA. 84.
Front Skirt
Left Apron left plain.
Tilt
Right Apron goes under the left and is plain
DIA. 87.
THE HIGHLAND DOUBLET, VEST, & KILT.
Left or Top Apron
DIA. 86.
Right or Under Skirt

112

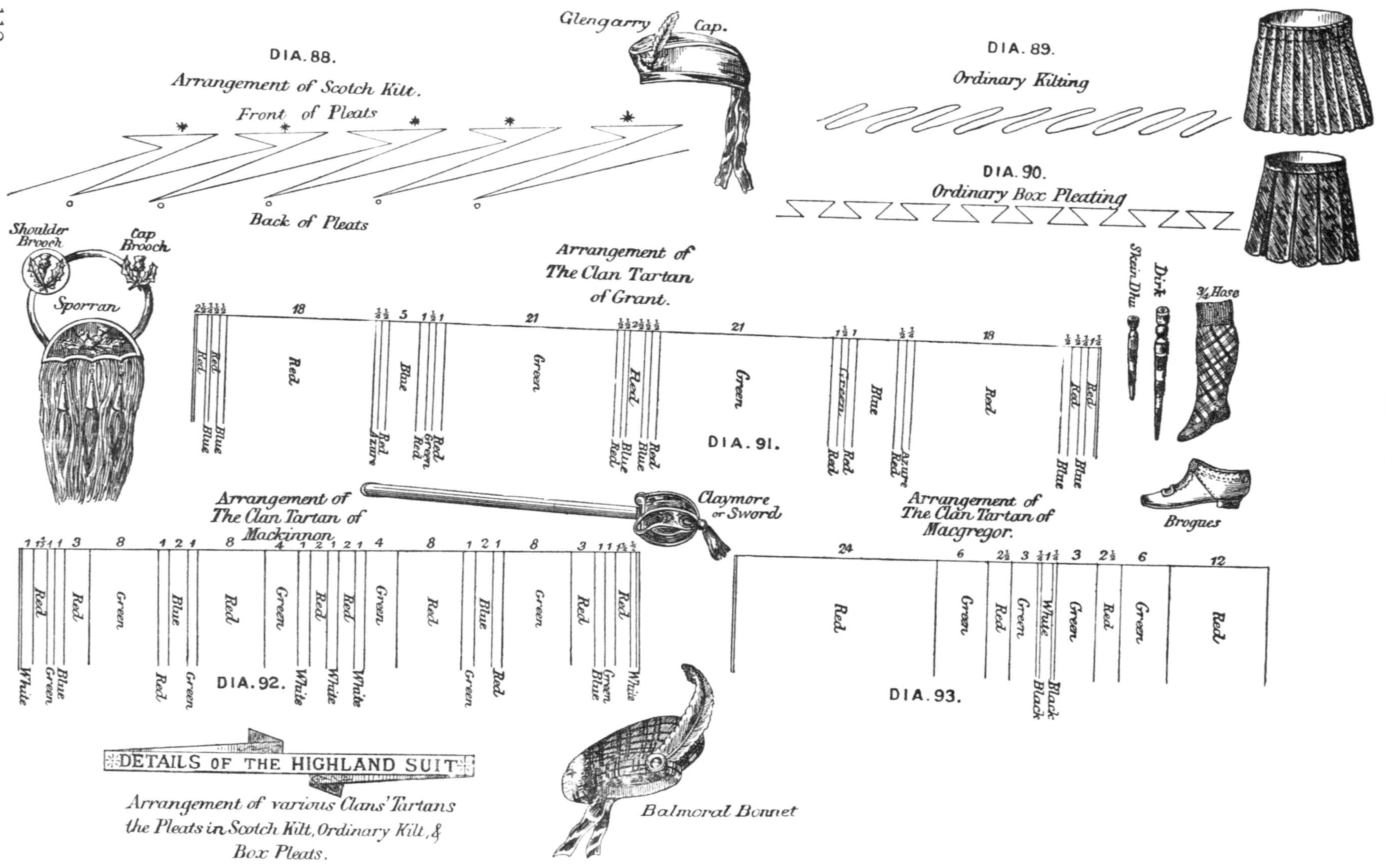

Glengarry Cap.
DIA. 88.
Arrangement of Scotch Kilt.
Front of Pleats
Back of Pleats
Shoulder Brooch
Cap Brooch
Sporran
DIA. 89.
Ordinary Kilting
DIA. 90.
Ordinary Box Pleating
Skein Dhu
Dirk
¾ Hose
Brogues
Arrangement of
The Clan Tartan
of Grant.
Red
Red
Blue
Blue
Red
Blue
Red
Azure
Green
Red
Green
Red
Green
Red
Blue
Red
Green
Blue
Red
Green
Red
Blue
Azure
Red
Red
Blue
Blue
DIA. 91.
Arrangement of
The Clan Tartan of
Mackinnon
Claymore or Sword
Arrangement of
The Clan Tartan of
Macgregor.
Red
White
Red
Green
Blue
Green
Red
Blue
Green
Red
Red
White
Red
White
Green
White
Red
Green
Blue
Green
Red
Red
Green
Blue
White
DIA. 92.
Red
Green
Red
Green
White
Black
Black
Green
Red
Green
Red
DIA. 93.
DETAILS OF THE HIGHLAND SUIT
Arrangement of various Clans' Tartans
the Pleats in Scotch Kilt, Ordinary Kilt, &
Box Pleats.
Balmoral Bonnet

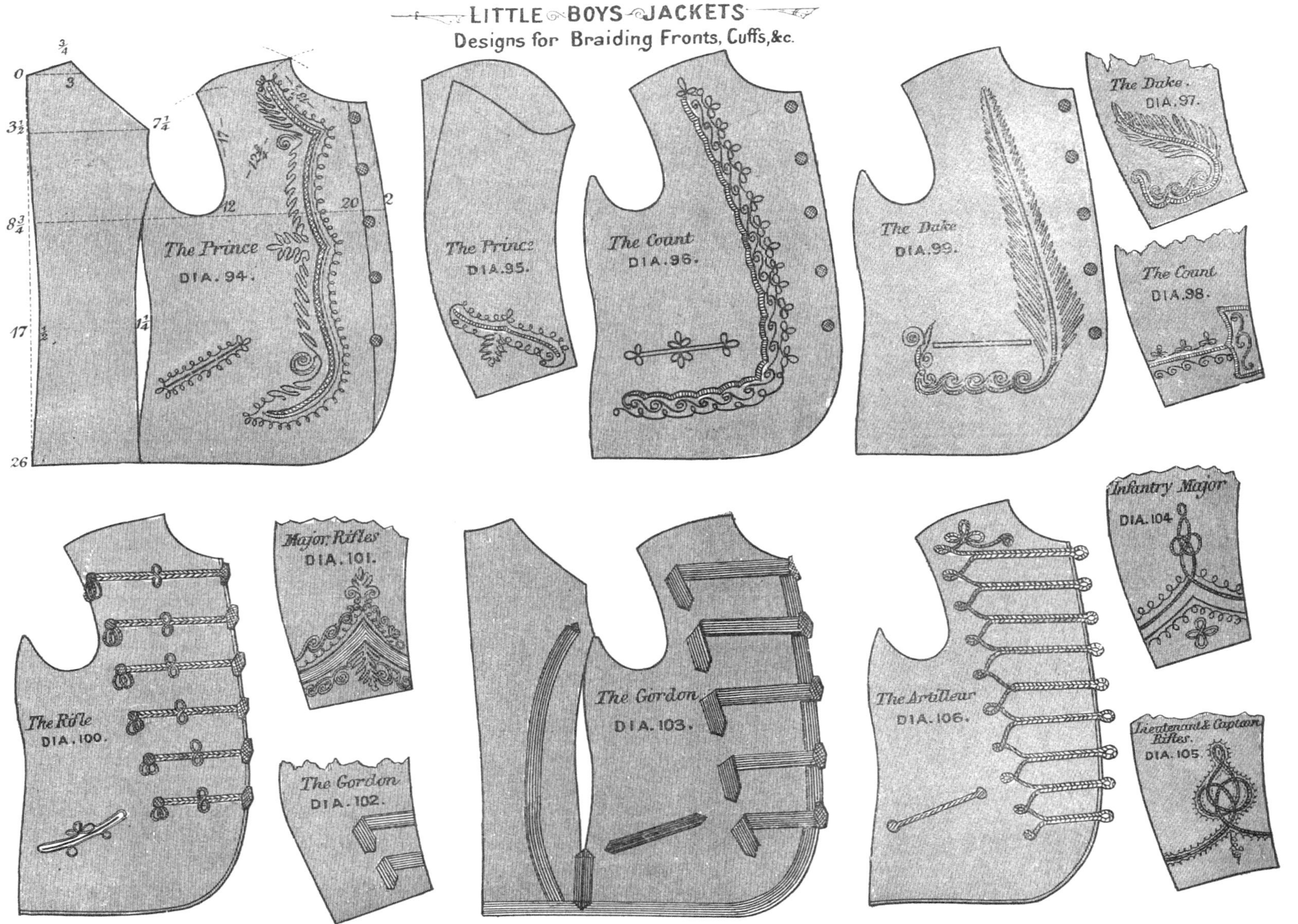
The Prince
DIA. 94.
The Prince
DIA. 95.
The Count
DIA. 96.
The Duke.
DIA. 99.
The Duke.
DIA. 97.
The Count
DIA. 98.
The Rifle
DIA. 100.
Major Rifles
DIA. 101.
The Gordon
DIA. 102.
The Gordon
DIA. 103.
The Artillear
DIA. 106.
Infantry Major
DIA. 104.
Lieutenant & Captain
Rifles.
DIA. 105.

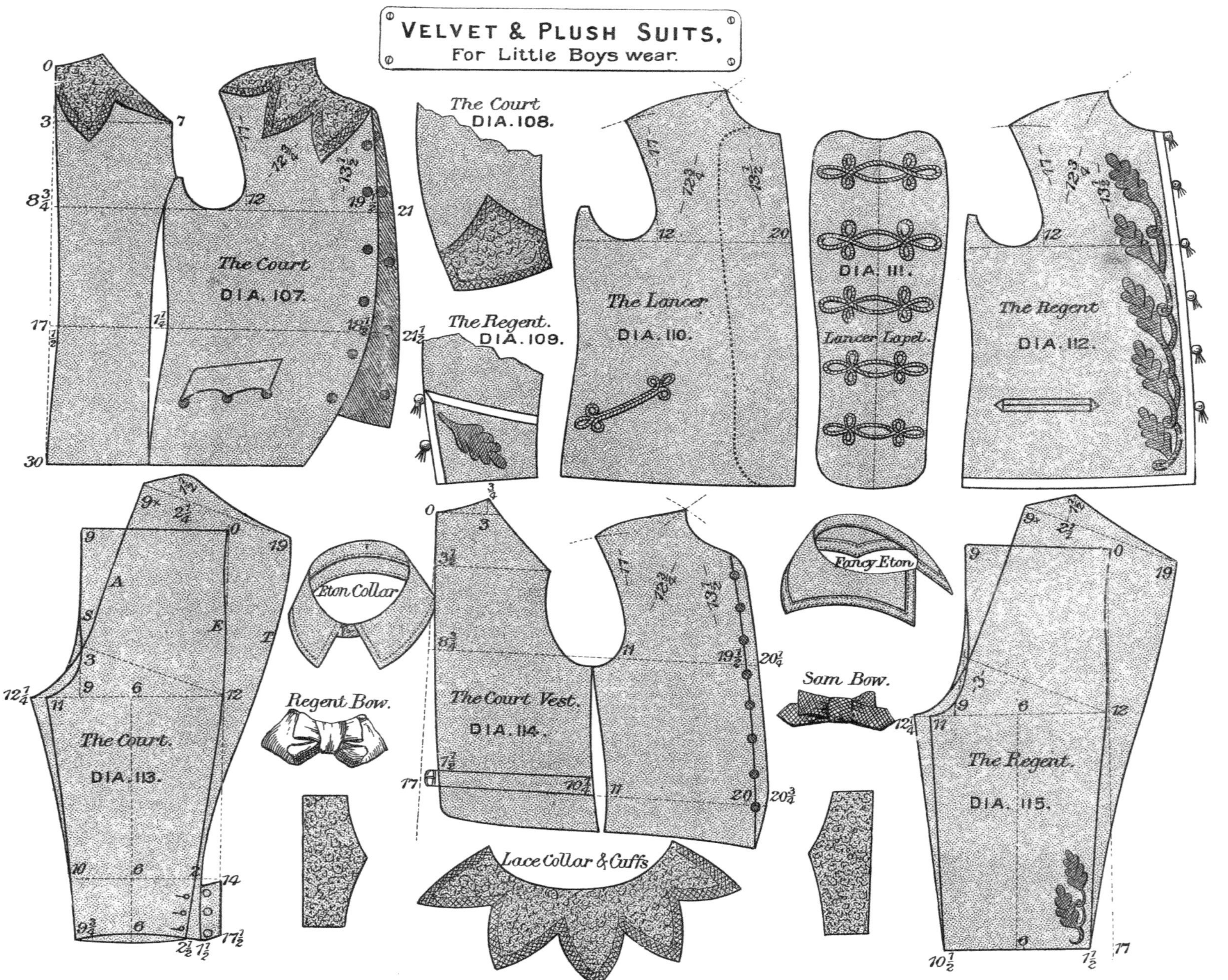

VELVET & PLUSH SUITS,
For Little Boys wear.
The Court DIA. 107.
The Court DIA. 108.
The Regent. DIA. 109.
The Lancer DIA. 110.
DIA. 111.
Lancer Lapel.
The Regent DIA. 112.
The Court. DIA. 113.
Eton Collar
Regent Bow.
The Court Vest. DIA. 114.
Fancy Eton
Sam Bow.
The Regent. DIA. 115.
Lace Collar & Cuffs

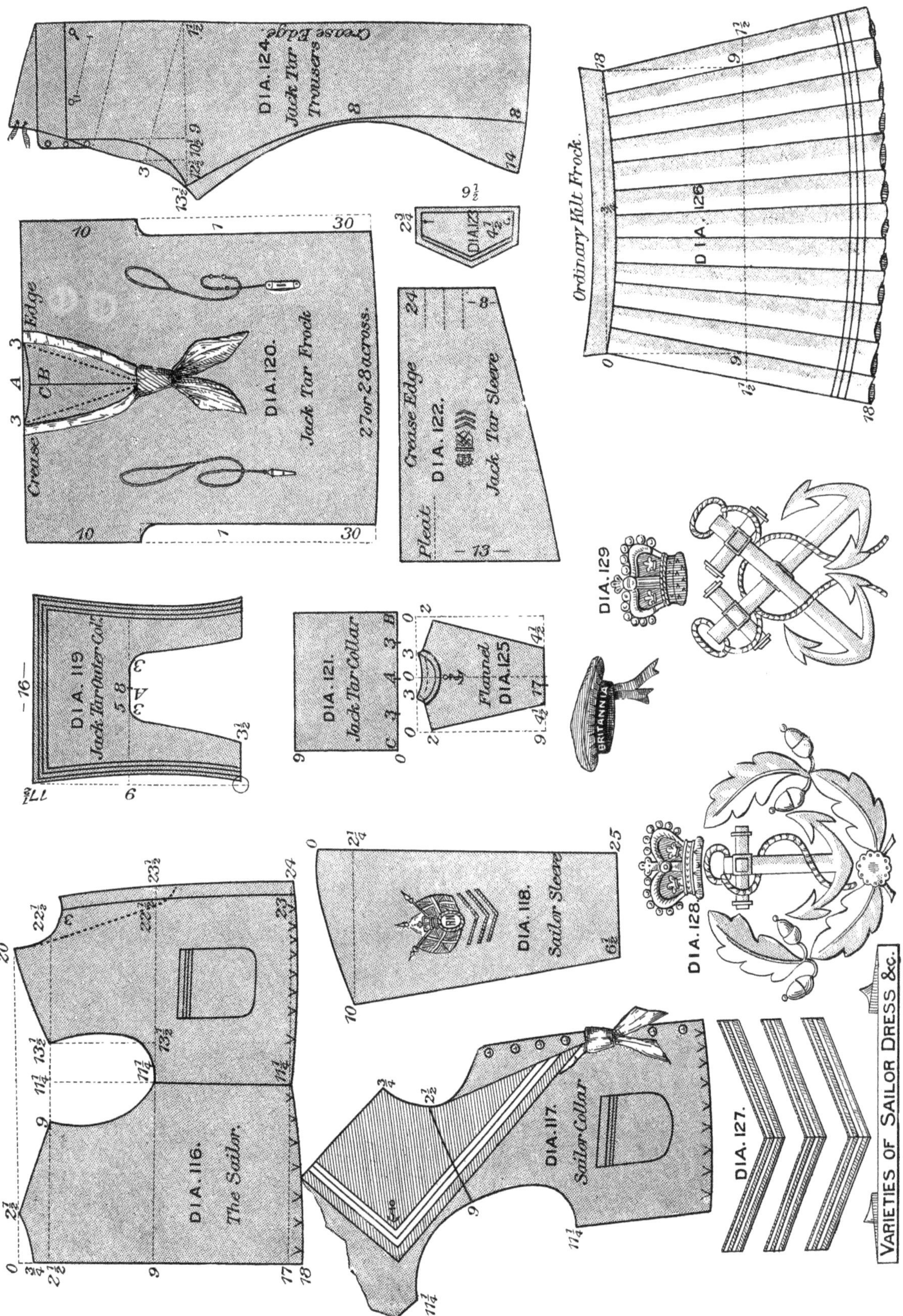
Crease Edge
DIA.124.
Jack Tar Trousers
DIA.123.
Ordinary Kilt Frock.
DIA.126.
DIA.120.
Jack Tar Frock.
27 or 28 across.
Crease Edge
Edge
Crease
Crease Edge
DIA.122.
Jack Tar Sleeve
Pleat
DIA.129.
DIA.119.
Jack Tar Outer Col.
DIA.121.
Jack Tar Collar
Flannel
DIA.125.
BRITANNIA
DIA.128.
DIA.116.
The Sailor.
DIA.118.
Sailor Sleeve
DIA.117.
Sailor Collar
DIA.127.
VARIETIES OF SAILOR DRESS &c.

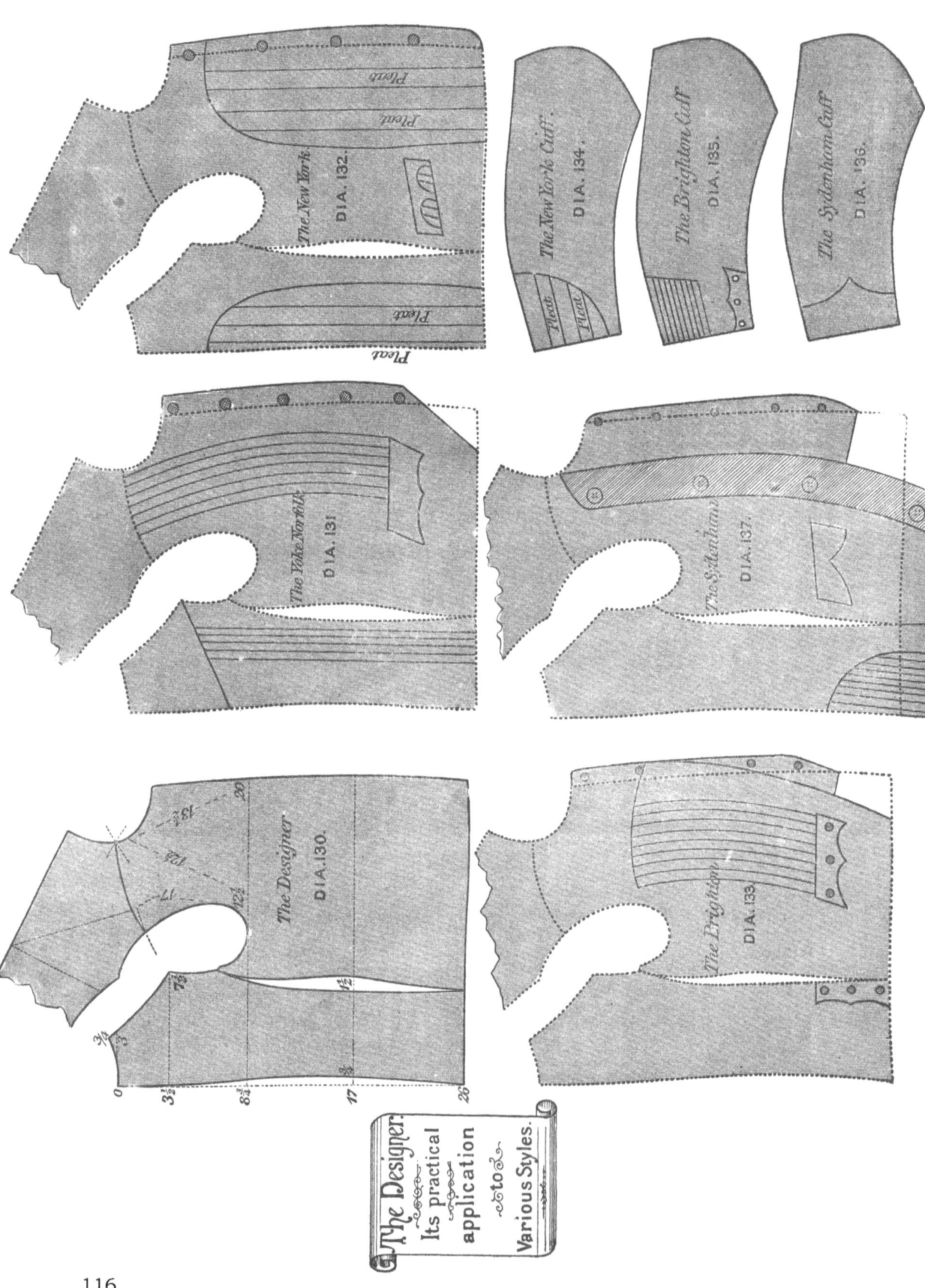
Pleat
Pleat
The New York.
DIA. 132.
Pleat
Pleat
The New York Cuff.
DIA. 134.
Pleat
Pleat
The Brighton Cuff
DIA. 135.
The Sydenham Cuff
DIA. 136.
The Yoke Norfolk
DIA. 131
The Sydenham
DIA. 137.
The Designer
DIA. 130.
The Brighton
DIA. 133.
The Designer
Its practical
application
Various Styles.

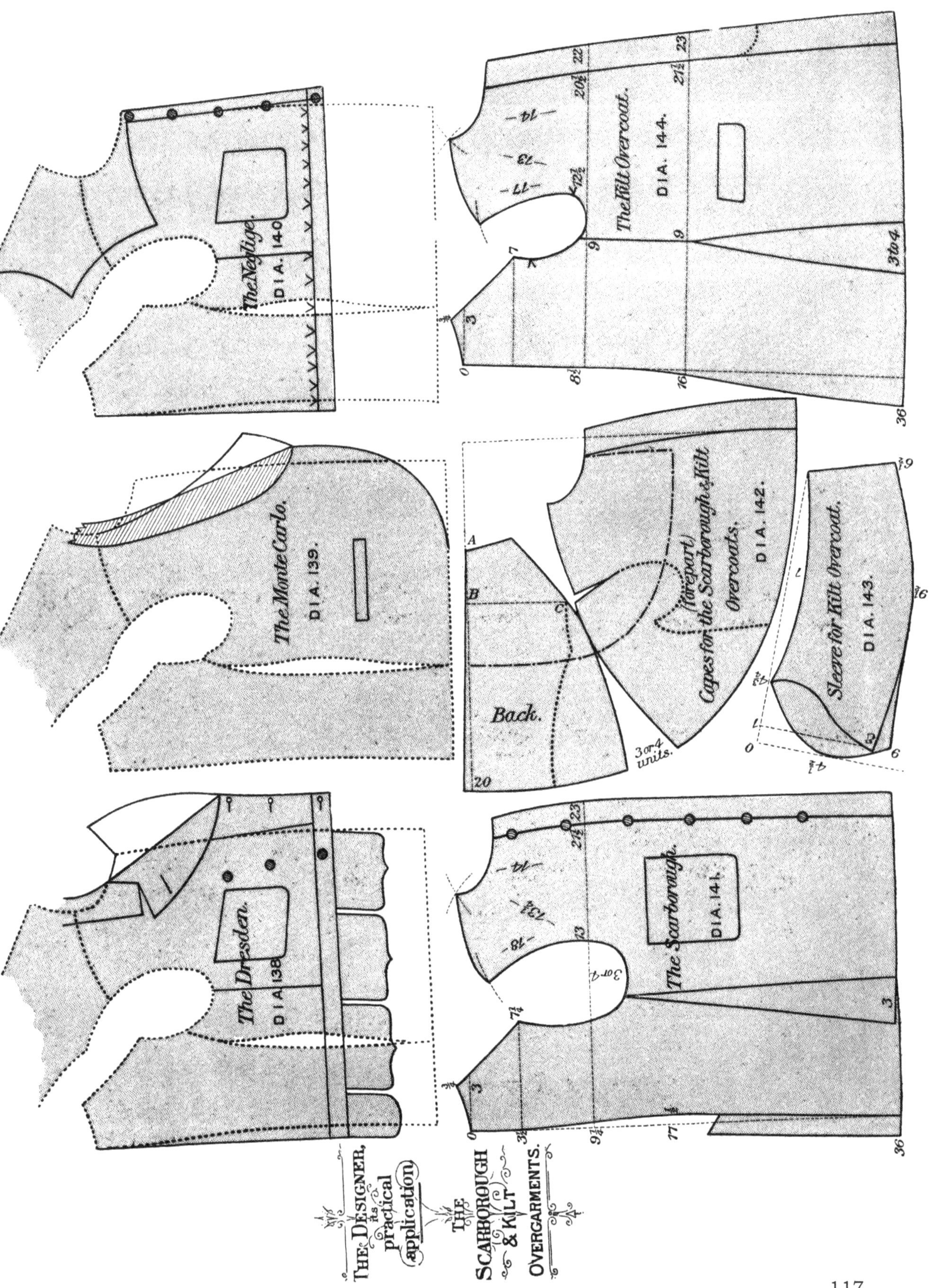

The Negligee.
D.I.A. 140.
The Monte Carlo.
D.I.A. 139.
The Dresden.
D.I.A. 138.
The Kilt Overcoat.
D.I.A. 144.
Back.
3 or 4 units.
(Forepart)
Capes for the Scarborough & Kilt Overcoats.
D.I.A. 142.
Sleeve for Kilt Overcoat.
D.I.A. 143.
The Scarborough.
D.I.A. 141.
THE DESIGNER, its practical application
THE SCARBOROUGH & KILT OVERGARMENTS.

118

STRAIGHTNESS & CROOKEDNESS &c.
THE AUSTRIAN.
DIA. 145.
"THE REAL LITTLE LORD FAUNTELROY."
DIA. 146.
LEGGINGS.
DIA. 147.
How a Crooked Shoulder
may be produced
DIA. 151.
To produce ease in scye.
DIA. 148.
Straightness & Crookedness.
of Shoulder.
DIA. 149.
Length of Front Edge.
NOT
Straightness & Crookedness.
of Shoulder.
DIA. 150.

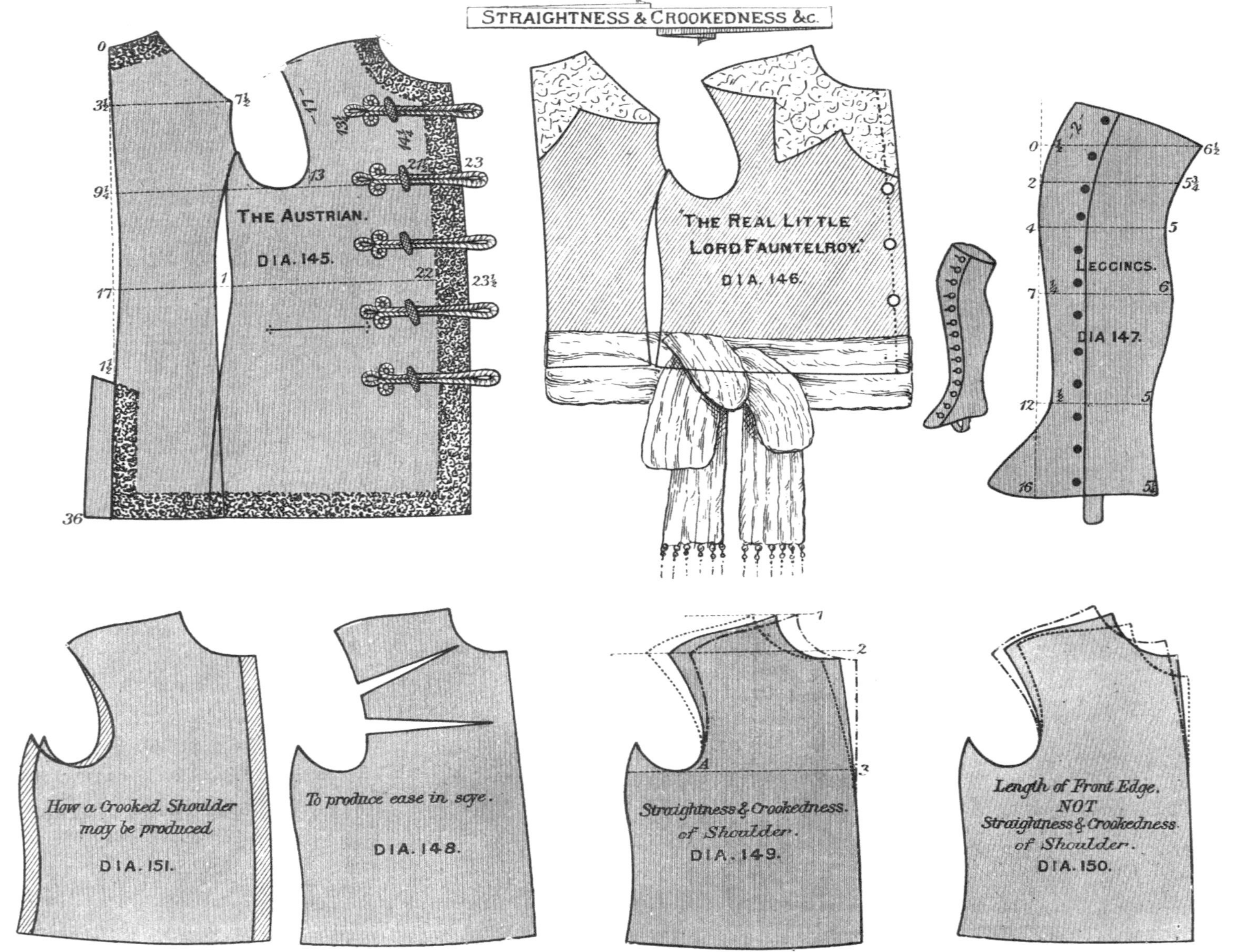

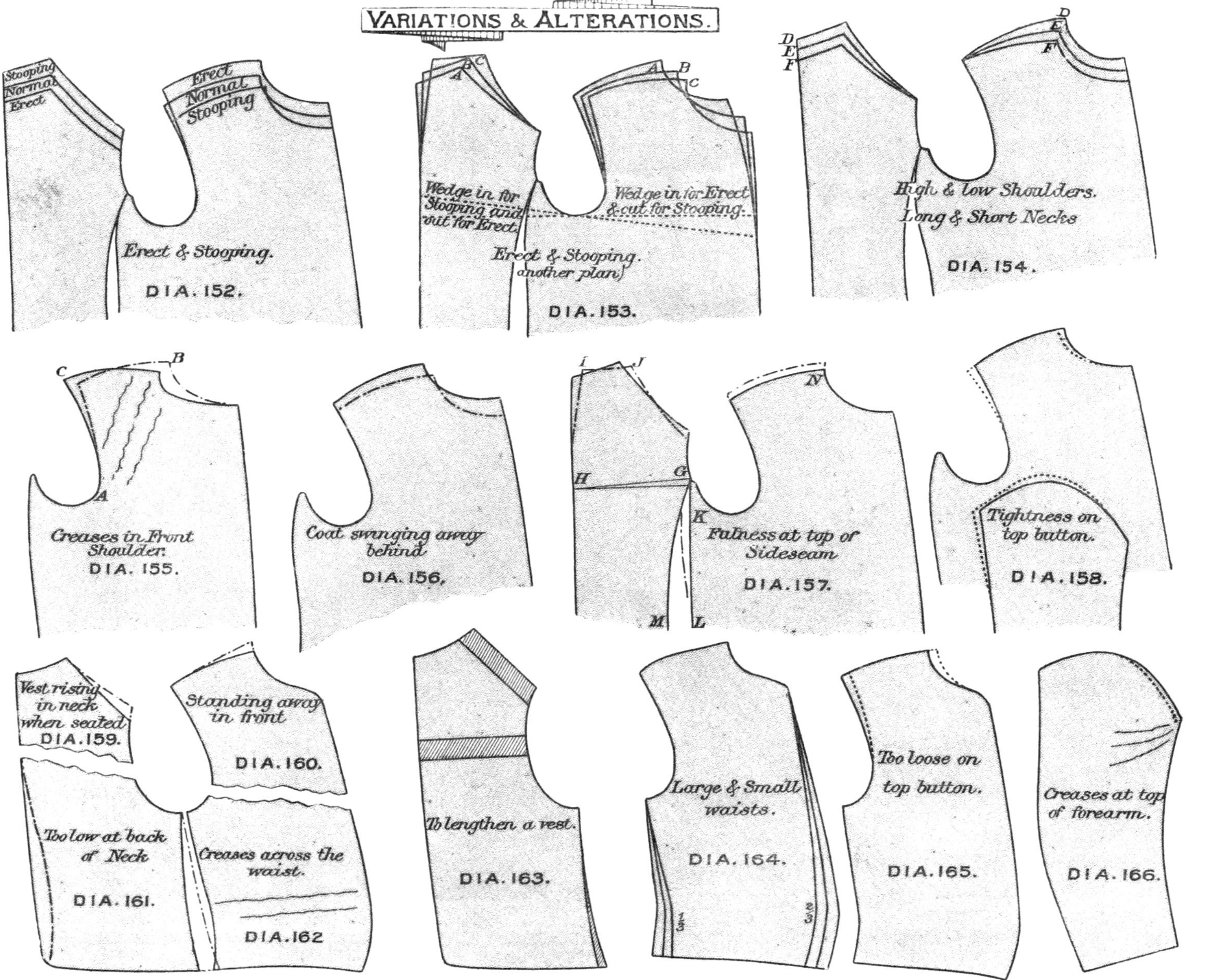

VARIATIONS & ALTERATIONS.
Stooping
Normal
Erect
Erect
Normal
Stooping
Erect & Stooping.
DIA. 152.
Wedge in for
Stooping and
cut for Erect.
Wedge in for Erect
& cut for Stooping.
Erect & Stooping.
(another plan)
DIA. 153.
High & low Shoulders.
Long & Short Necks
DIA. 154.
Creases in Front
Shoulder.
DIA. 155.
Coat swinging away
behind
DIA. 156.
Fulness at top of
Sideseam
DIA. 157.
Tightness on
top button.
DIA. 158.
Vest rising
in neck
when seated
DIA. 159.
Standing away
in front
DIA. 160.
Too low at back
of Neck
DIA. 161.
Creases across the
waist.
DIA. 162
To lengthen a vest.
DIA. 163.
Large & Small
waists.
DIA. 164.
Too loose on
top button.
DIA. 165.
Creases at top
of forearm.
DIA. 166.

WELT
FOREPART
A
UNDERSLEEVE BACK
TOP SLEEVE
FLY
A
TOPSIDES
UNDERSIDES
VEST
B
B
B
B
WELT

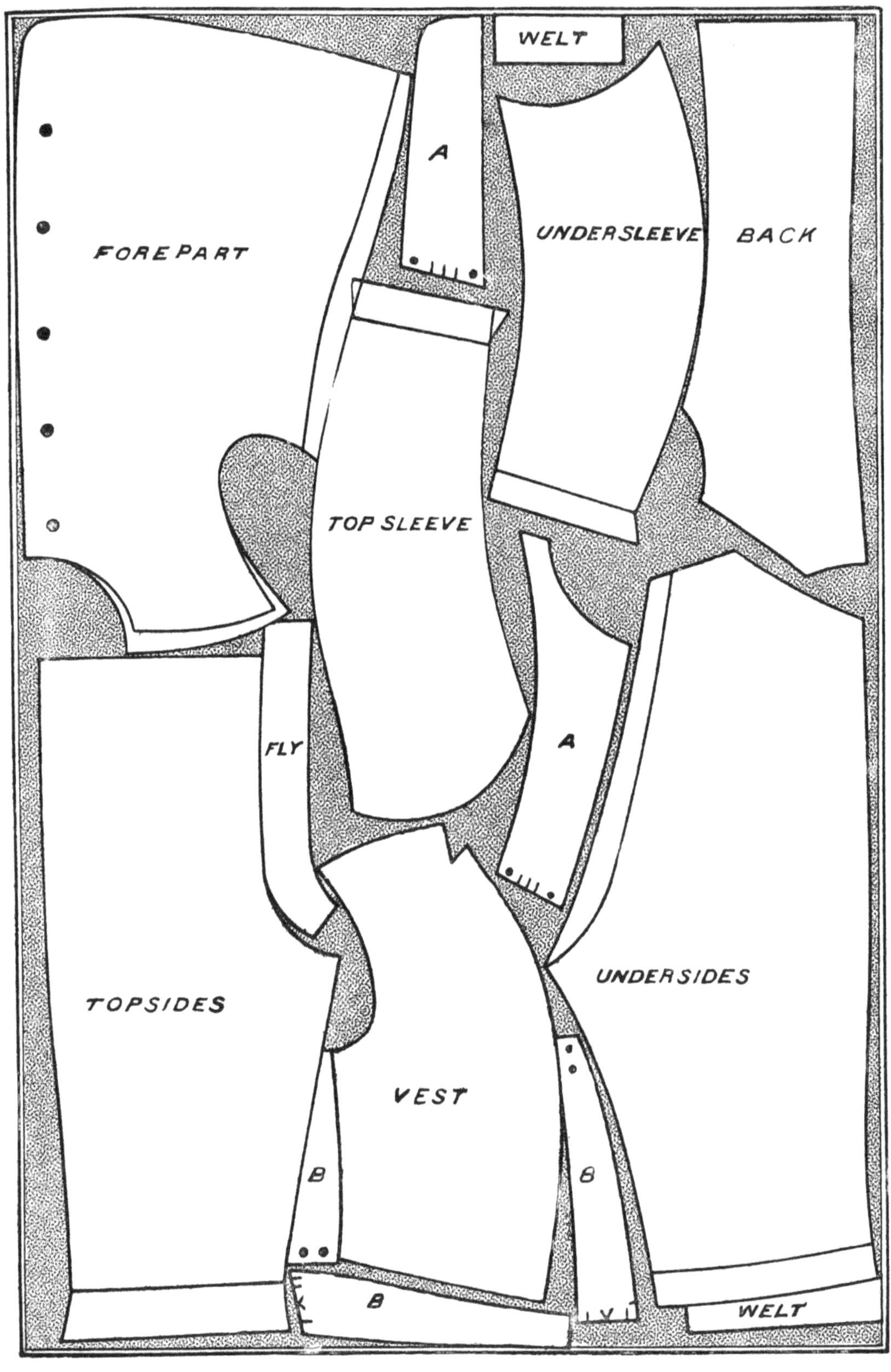

DIAGRAM 168.

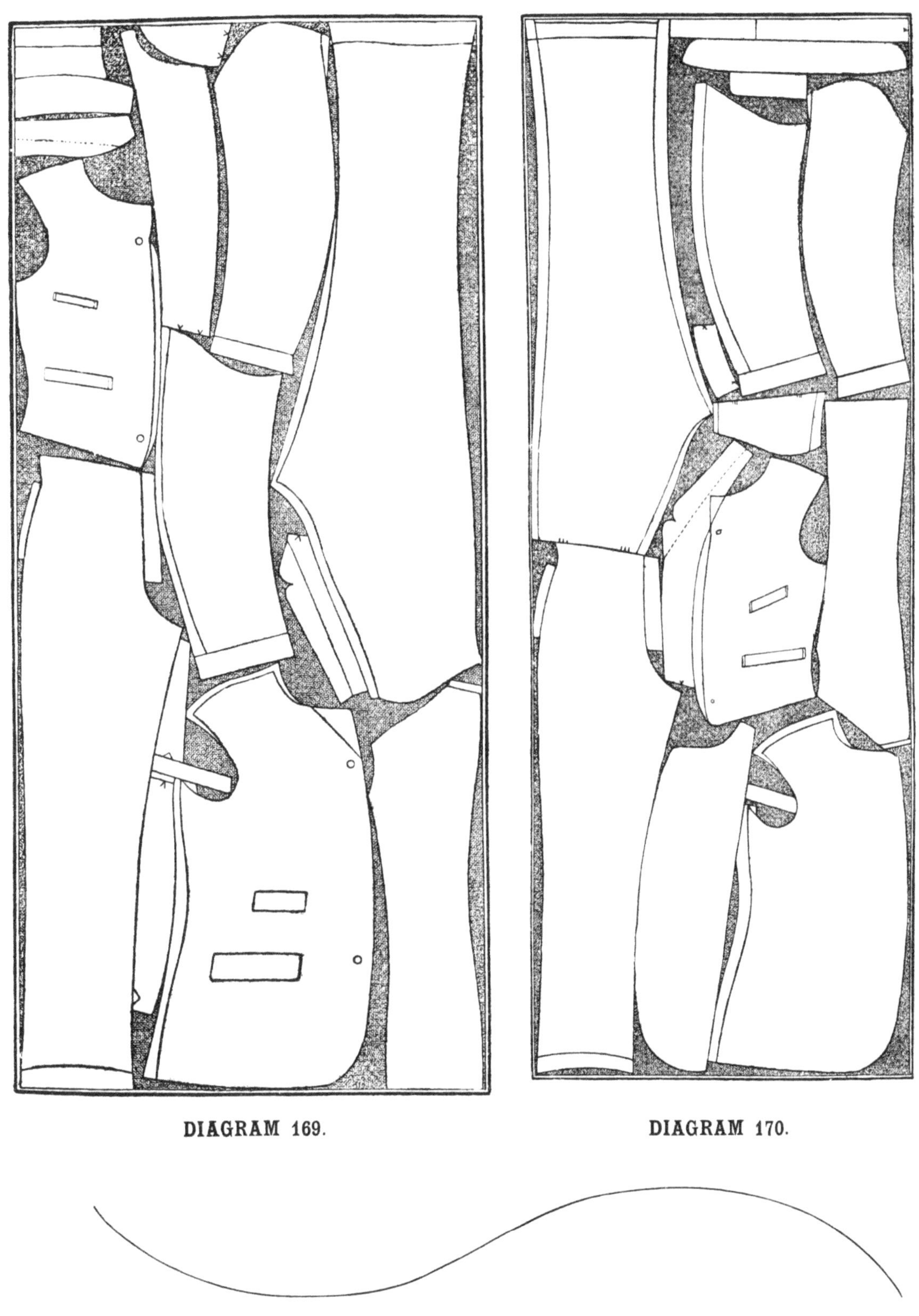

DIAGRAM 169.

DIAGRAM 170.

THE LINE OF BEAUTY.—DIAGRAM 171.-